AGNEW: PROFILE IN CONFLICT

AGNEW: PROFILE IN CONFLICT

Jim G. Lucas

AWARD BOOKS
NEW YORK

TANDEM BOOKS
LONDON

Distributed by Charles Scribner's Sons • New York

A—5.70(C)

Printed in the United States of America
Library of Congress Catalog Card Number 70-124445

ACKNOWLEDGMENTS

Once my curiosity about Spiro T. Agnew became aroused it was not easily satisfied. It took the cooperation of many, some of whom did not know me and had no particular reason to help, to write this book. To them, I am particularly grateful. I like to think they, too, felt that we all needed to know more about the Vice-President whose name suddenly *was* a Household Word.

I am indebted to many, especially to the Vice-President himself, for taking time from a crushing schedule to talk with me; to Herb Thompson, his able press secretary and now my good friend; to Cynthia Rosenwald, even though I still make her nervous; to Herb Klein, the Presidential communications director; and to Bryce Harlow, my fellow Oklahoman, a White House assistant who I think must have vouched for me.

I am indebted to others like former Governor McKeldin of Maryland; Circuit Judges Lester Barrett and Albert Menchine; to Sam Kimmel, Mr. Agnew's law partner, whose fund of Agnew lore was most useful; to the staff of the *Towson* (Maryland) *Jeffersonian,* who opened their files to me; to the *Evening Capital* for the use of their files in Annapolis; and to Clewell Howell, an assistant Baltimore County state's attorney who, for reasons I never understood but never questioned, helped me find what I needed in musty records stored deep in the courthouse basement or high up in the attic.

My thanks go to Earl Richert, my editor-in-chief, and to Jack Steele, my managing editor, for giving me the time; to David Stolberg, managing editor of the *Washington Daily News*; and to the staff of the Pratt Library in Baltimore, on whose time and facilities I made imposing demands. A special vote of thanks to Dick Maschi, the Scripps-Howard Newspaper Alliance librarian in Washington, and to Josephine Mockler, librarian for the *Washington Daily News,* both of whom suffered my rifling their files over weeks at a time.

And, finally, I express my deepest appreciation to my sister,

Mrs. George A. Moore, of Bowie, Maryland, without whose valuable research, wise counsel, and encouragement, this book could not have been written.

Jim G. Lucas

Washington, D.C.

CONTENTS

I. THE EARLY YEARS   9

Debut into Politics—Failure Can Be Lucky—Agnew the Elder—Spiro's School Years—Spiro and His Wife-To-Be—Agnew the Soldier—New Job Responsibilities

II. LABOR LAWYER   19

Towson and a New Way of Life—Agnew's First Law Cases—Accused of Incompetence—PTA Participation—Where the First Labor Law Case Led—The Menhaden Fishermen—Agnew's First Political Victory

III. THE BREAKTHROUGH   28

Baltimore County's Democratic Machine—Appointment to the Board of Zoning Appeals—How Agnew Became County Executive—Accomplishments Between 1962-1968

IV. ANNAPOLIS   38

The Gubernatorial Nomination—Agnew's Opponents—The Campaign and Its Issues—The Family in Annapolis—Agnew as Governor—Battle of the Peanut Butter Jars—Civil Disruption—Agnew's Confrontation With the Blacks—The Constitutional Convention and Its Outcome

V. SEARCH FOR A CANDIDATE   63

Agnew and the '68 Presidential Election—The "Draft Rockefeller Campaign"—Agnew's First Meeting With Nixon—Agnew Nominates Nixon—The Miami Convention—Agnew in Miami

VI. SURPRISE CHOICE   77

How a Vice-President is Chosen—The Candidates for the Number-two Spot—Qualities Nixon Looked For—Agnew Gets the Big News—First Press Conference As Vice-President—Republican Reaction to Agnew's Nomination—John

Lindsay's Convention Speech For Agnew—Black Reaction
To Agnew as Vice-President—How Spiro Campaigned—Campaign-Fund Secret—"The Fat Jap"

VII. A TARGET   92

The Charges Against Agnew—First Run-In With *The New
York Times*—The Polls and the Republicans—How Nixon
and Agnew Accepted the Outcome

VIII. VICE-PRESIDENT   100

History of the Vice-Presidency—Giving Up the Governorship—The Agnews Move to Washington—The Nixon-Agnew
Relationship—Agnew's Responsibilities—Tour of Southeast
Asia—Criticism at Home—Anti-American Demonstrations—
Agnew in Vietnam—Kim and the Moratorium—Nixon Compared to Agnew—"Effete Snobs"—Public Response to Vice-
Presidential Speeches—Agnew and the Senate

IX. AGNEW VERSUS THE MEDIA   116

Kennedy, Harriman and Agnew—Vice-Presidential Views on
Desegregation—Agnew Attacks Television News Commentators—The Networks' Response—Effects of Agnew's Views on
TV News—The Vice-President and the Major Newspapers—
The *New York Times'* Response

X. AGNEW TODAY—A POTPOURRI   132

White House Romance—Health Considerations of the Vice-
President—Agnew and the Washington Social Scene—The
Agnew Family Roots—The Vice-President's Personal Friends
—Agnew's Daily Routine—How Agnew Serves Nixon—The
Vice-President's Staff—Agnew as Politician—LBJ and the
Vice-President—Agnew Analyzes Himself—The Secret Service—Vice-Presidential Duties—Those Who Serve Agnew—
Has Agnew Changed?—The Vice-President's Future

INDEX   153

I

THE EARLY YEARS

Spiro T. Agnew's debut into politics was a total disaster. In 1960 he decided to run for a fifteen-year term as associate circuit judge. He placed fifth in a field of five. Even the other Republican in a nonpartisan contest ran well ahead. Agnew got 49,764 votes. Judge James J. Lindsay got 138,-602. Judge George M. Berry drew 112,843, and Judge W. Albert Menchine, 106,517.

"I'm one of three men who can say they've beaten Ted in a political race," says Judge Menchine, a bouncy little man whose son broadcasts the Washington Senators baseball games. Menchine and Agnew are now close friends.

Agnew and his friends concede the race was a mistake.

"You should never run against a sitting judge," admitted Sam Kimmel, Ted Agnew's law partner, campaign manager, and long-time friend.

It was also one of the luckiest breaks Agnew ever had. Had he been elected to the circuit bench in 1960, he would still have been hearing divorce cases and delinquency complaints in Towson, Maryland—with eight years remaining to serve—when Richard M. Nixon looked around and chose him for his running mate at Miami Beach, Florida, in 1968.

By now this is accepted, matter of factly, in Towson as part of the Agnew mystique, the Horatio Alger rags-to-riches story written long ago. Only the script remains to be acted out.

People in Towson today speak of Ted Agnew with awe.

The odds against him from the start were incredible.

The prospects that he—a Republican, and a lower-echelon one at that—might attain political honors seemed remote.

Yet he sought them all—hungrily, eagerly—and he won.

Spiro Theodore Agnew was born in Baltimore, Maryland, on November 9, 1918. His father, Theodore Spiro Agnew (father's and son's names are reversed) was a Greek imi-

9

grant who came to this country when he was 21. He remained to become a leader of the Baltimore Greek community and a power of sorts in the local Democratic party. The father remained a Democrat until his son was inaugurated as Baltimore County executive in 1962. Then 82, he died a few months later.

Agnew the elder was a native of Gargalianos, Messenia, Greece, a member of the Anagnostopoulos family; the name was later shortened to Agnew.

Agnew remembers his father telling him their family had been "quite well to do," that it had owned large olive groves in the hills around Gargalianos and had prospered. His father is dead now, and Agnew is not clear what happened to their property in Greece. But there was either a depression or the olive crops failed and the family was wiped out.

At the turn of the century, in 1899, Theodore Spiro Anagnostopoulos decided to emigrate to the United States. He did not come immediately to Baltimore. Instead, he settled in Boston—where his ship had docked—and looked for a job.

Young Anagnostopoulos spoke no English. Most jobs were barred to him for that reason. Fortunately, however, there was a growing Greek colony in Boston. Its members were close-knit, well-organized, and prepared to help their own.

One friend ran a barbershop. Agnew's father had never cut a head of hair in his life, but he was taken in and given a chair. His first few jobs must have been sheer terror for him, and worse for the customers. Again, fortunately, the majority were of Greek origin and tolerant of the young man's mistakes.

He proved a quick learner, an apt pupil. Soon he was cutting hair, shaving faces, with the best of them.

With his advancement in craftmanship came a quick mastery of English. At least he could make himself understood.

He soon left the barbershop to open a lunchroom. It was not a big one. Young Anagnostopoulos specialized in box lunches for Boston's workingmen, the dockhands, the streetcar conductors, and the cops. The Irish among them soon learned they got their money's worth from the cheerful young Greek who so badly mangled the King's English. He did a good, though hardly a land-office, business.

Like most Greeks, Anagnostopoulos was a frugal man. He

saved his money. Eventually, in 1912, he moved on to Baltimore.

He had heard of that port city from the Boston sailors and it appealed to him. Boston's winters were cruelly harsh, particularly for someone used to a warmer climate. Often he longed to return to Greece and his olive groves. Baltimore seemed ideal. situated as it was—or so he had heard—in the sunny South.

In Baltimore he invested in a restaurant that he called the Brighton. He did something else: He went to court and changed his family name to Aganost. This was later shortened to Agnew—and Agnew it would remain until in later years it became a household word in the United States.

Agnew the elder soon sold the Brighton, which had done well, and opened a larger, more exclusive eating place on Howard Street. It was called the Picadilly.

It is typical of the practical man he was that he never specialized in Greek cuisine. There were not very many Greeks in Baltimore, and those who lived there more often than not preferred to eat at home. Baltimoreans who dined out liked their lobster and crabcakes, their steaks, chops, and potatoes—and that is what he gave them.

Again, business prospered.

Among the first friends Agnew's father made after he moved to Baltimore was a Dr. William Pollard, a respected veterinarian, and his wife, the former Margaret Akers. of Bristol, Virginia. They often dined at the Brighton, and then at the Picadilly. Agnew always saw that they got the best of service.

A lovely southern belle whose quiet charms impressed the young Greek and did not fade with the passage of time, Mrs. Pollard became Mrs. Agnew when Dr. Pollard died a few years after their first meeting. She and Dr. Pollard had had one son, who was eleven years old when his stepbrother Spiro was born, in 1918.

W. Roy Pollard, an insurance man, still lives in the Baltimore area. Pollard and Agnew still correspond, and Roy apparently follows Spiro's speeches with interest. After New Orleans, he sent him a note saying, "That was a great one!"

Spiro Agnew went through adolescence and grew into manhood during the Depression years. That experience left its mark on him and explains, in part, his impatience with those he now considers whiners and cry-babies.

Ted—as he was to be called later—was a tall, awkward boy, with a diffidence bordering on shyness. He was six feet tall by the time he was thirteen. But he was lean and lank and his scarecrow physique embarrassed him. Once, when looking over an album of family photographs, he winced when he came across the picture of himself as a teen-ager. "Thank God," he said, "I put on weight later."

The family had moved to the Forest Park area of Baltimore, and young Spiro attended, successively, Public school 69, Garrison Junior High School, and Forest Park High School.

His school career was not particularly remarkable. His grades were average. He joined no political clubs and appeared, as a young man, to have no particular set of political convictions. He smoked a pipe briefly to impress the girls—but soon gave it up. He was not involved in athletics: an innate awkwardness and an aversion to being shown up kept him away from the playing fields. If anything distinguished him, it was an ability to express himself forcefully and with clarity.

By now his father was actively involved, not only as a precinct worker for the Democratic party—enjoying a talking acquaintance with the great and near great of Baltimore—but also as a pillar of the Greek community. He frequently was asked to speak for the party and as a leader of his ethnic group.

From the time Spiro was fourteen, he wrote his father's speeches.

"You can say it better," the old man would say. "Write it out for me."

Meanwhile, however, the family business was failing. One of the first luxuries the middle class dispenses with in a depression is dining out. The Picadilly too often was empty. Reluctantly, for many of them were fellow Greeks, Agnew's father let go waiters, waitresses, and cooks in an attempt to keep the Picadilly alive.

He was doomed to defeat from the start. Eventually, the Picadilly was lost.

So was the warm, love-filled family home in Forest Park where Spiro and Roy, now on his own, had grown up. The family moved to a small apartment above a florist shop at Madison and Howard streets. Somehow, probably from his influential friends, many of whom were now as hard up as he, Spiro's father managed to get the money to buy an old truck. He would fill it with vegetables from the produce market and peddle them door to door. He made barely enough to keep the family going. Spiro helped after school.

Spiro Agnew remembers how hurt he was when neighbors casually referred to "that Greek family up the street." Classmates made crude jokes about his name. He vowed that, if he was a father, none of his children would have Greek names. He kept that promise. The Agnew children are named Pam, Randy, Susan, and Kim.

Proud as he was—and is—of his Greek heritage, Spiro Agnew is a stranger to his father's tongue. He has never particularly felt the need to learn Greek. But there was one occasion on which the lack became painful.

During his campaign for the Vice-Presidency, Agnew went to New York to confer with the wealthy Greek-American theater magnate Spyros Skouras about campaign funds. As Agnew entered his office, Skouras rose to greet him and spoke in his native tongue. Agnew had to confess, red-faced, he hadn't the slightest idea what Skouras was talking about.

During the Nixon-Agnew campaign, Agnew was often greeted by enthusiastic Greek-American supporters in the language of the homeland. He solved that problem by giving each a particularly firm handclasp, one hand over the other, and gazing deeply—almost soulfully—into the other's eyes as if to say, "Yes, brother, you and I share a secret bond."

Agnew was graduated from Forest Park High School in 1937. The school yearbook was dedicated that year to "progressivism," to the class's desire to alter the shape of the world it was to inherit. Agnew seemed an unlikely candidate to carry out that pledge. Yet he was later to gain a reputation, as Baltimore County executive, the third most important post in the state, as a progressive mover and shaker of established systems.

Meanwhile the family fortunes began to improve. Franklin D. Roosevelt was in Washington, money was being pumped into the economy, and the nation seemed back on the road to recovery.

Even as a fruit peddler, Spiro's father had managed to save a little. He was able, eventually, to open a third restaurant—this one called the Chesaco Inn—in the 3100 block of Pulaski Highway.

"It was out on the road to Philadelphia," Judge Menchine

recalls. "I often ate there. There was good food. and a comfortable cocktail lounge. And old man Agnew was a fine old man, a fine old man, indeed. The type you enjoyed being around."

Spiro enrolled at Baltimore's Johns Hopkins University as a chemistry major. But those were unsettled times. Another world war was approaching and America's young men knew that, sooner or later, they would be caught up in it. There was a general feeling of "live today, for tomorrow we may die." Agnew confesses now that he began more and more to neglect his studies and turn to other things. Moreover, while he enjoyed chemical theories, he detested laboratory work. It was messy, smelly, and alien to his nature.

Despite his financial recovery—once again he was being consulted by Baltimore's Democratic leaders as a ward leader and as a pillar in the Greek community—Agnew's father was not a wealthy man. He disliked throwing good money after bad. He was willing to finance his son's education, but he wanted results. And the results he saw disappointed him. Like many a father, before and after him, he told his only son to shape up or ship out.

After three years as a fledgling chemist, Agnew left Johns Hopkins.

Again, fate seemed to intervene. Spiro T. Agnew, chemist, would be an unlikely choice as Richard M. Nixon's running mate in 1968.

Agnew now says that he felt at the time that his abilities in English and writing were "more compatible with the law than with science." He transferred to the University of Baltimore Night Law School and found the studies more to his liking. Law fascinated him, as it still does.

To support himself—he was unwilling to depend entirely upon his father any longer—he took a job with the Maryland Casualty Company in Baltimore, as a legal aide.

Elinor Isabel Judefind—Judy to her friends—also worked at Maryland Casualty. She had grown up four blocks from this tall, well-groomed young man, but they had never met.

Spiro spotted her immediately. Whether by accident or design, he was "always tripping over me in the file room," she smiles.

Petite and dainty, Judy was the daughter of Dr. and Mrs. W. Lee Judefind. Dr. Judefind, a chemist, was vice-president of the Davison Chemical Company in Baltimore.

She was aware of the young aide's interest in her.

Agnew had little time—too little, he felt—for courtship, what with working for Maryland Casualty by day and studying law at night. But he applied himself. Their dates probably seem square to today's young. On their first, they went to the movies and had chocolate milk shakes at a drive-in. Ted then took Judy home and excused himself; he had to study. There was a great deal more of the same. There were a few double dates with other young couples, bowling games, and movies. Occasionally they dined out.

He was doing well in the office, but once again his grades were beginning to slip. It was the war, of course. The draft board was blowing hot on his neck. In September he was drafted into the Army—at twenty-one dollars a month.

To backtrack, shortly after he met his future wife, Agnew was promoted to the job of assistant underwriter in the Sprinkler Leakage and Water Damage Division of Maryland Casualty. He had an office, and a secretary, and the munificent salary of thirteen dollars a week. By the time he was drafted he was making eighteen dollars a week. In those days that was not bad.

December 7, 1941—Pearl Harbor Day—shattered his plans as it did for so many others.

Agnew had proposed and Judy had accepted. Eagerly they had planned their wedding. It was to be during his Christmas leave.

But after Pearl Harbor there were no leaves. The training schedule at Camp Croft, South Carolina, where he was stationed, was speeded up. Soon after Pearl Harbor, Agnew was spotted as potential officer material and transferred to Fort Knox, Kentucky, for officer training.

On May 24, 1942, he was graduated as a full-fledged second lieutenant in the armored corps. Judy came down for the event and three days later, on May 27, they were married back in Baltimore.

After a short honeymoon, Judy followed him back to Fort Knox, where she planned to stay until he went overseas. It was, by any reckoning, a miserable, hand-to-mouth existence. But the young couple, deeply in love, seemed not to know that. For them it was fun. To be together, however briefly, was enough.

Their homes, if they could be called that, were a succession of huts, hovels, and bug-infested motel rooms, sometimes little better than chicken coops, the kind of thing foisted off on married officers and their wives by greedy landlords in wartime.

Eventually, however, they managed to locate a garage apartment in Elizabethtown, Kentucky. Judy was in heaven. Ted was delighted simply because Judy was. With what she could manage from a shavetail's salary she bought the frilly curtains, the throw rugs—the little things that made it seem like a home.

Then another blow fell.

Agnew was ordered to Fort Campbell, Kentucky.

Judy followed, living in rented rooms until May, when she went back to Baltimore to have Pam, by that time only two months away. Her man soon went overseas.

Spiro Agnew was the kind of soldier most Americans are, the kind that win wars, take off their uniforms and go home, grateful the job is behind them.

He was assigned to the 10th Armored Division and rose to command one of its companies. He received the Combat Infantryman's Badge and the Bronze Star. No citation accompanied the awards. They handed out Bronze Stars rather freely in those days, and Agnew has never made a big thing out of it.

In the fall of 1944 he was moved to a post near Birmingham, England, and in December 1944, was assigned to invasion forces at Metz, France, with the Fifth Armored Infantry Battalion in the 10th Combat Command "B."

This was the first unit sent by the late Lt. General George S. Patton, Jr., to lift the siege of Tony McAuliffe's division at Bastogne during the Battle of the Bulge. Agnew's company saw action there. It was at Bastogne that he received the Combat Infantryman's Badge.

Demobilization, and Captain Agnew headed back to Baltimore and his family. He was fired with a new determination to make something of himself. With a wife and family— James Rand joined Pam in 1946—he was sobered by his new responsibilities.

He went back to Baltimore University to complete his law studies and was graduated in 1947. He worked at night as a part-time law clerk with one of the city's major firms, Smith and Barrett. His salary was twenty-five dollars a week, beefed up by a twenty-five-dollar on-the-job-training allowance from the GI Bill of Rights. It wasn't much to keep a family.

Things were tough. But they would have been tougher without Agnew's father. The old man was pulling what strings he could. It was at his request that a mutual friend, George Oursler, introduced Spiro at Smith and Barrett. One of the partners, E. Lester Barrett, now senior circuit judge in Baltimore County, was impressed by the young law student.

Spiro was working for Smith and Barrett when he graduated in 1947. Once he left school, his GI Bill payments stopped. Smith and Barrett could not raise him to the fifty dollars a week he needed, so he opened a law office of his own. If he found a single client he doesn't remember it. Hard up, he signed on with the Lumberman Mutual Insurance Company at $3,000 a year.

Michael Paul Smith and E. Lester Barrett remained his friends. Both were Republicans, aligned with the progressive wing of the party headed by then Governor Theodore Roosevelt McKeldin.

As soon as he left the service, Agnew had registered as a Democrat. He was not active politically, but his father was a Democrat at the ward level and it seemed the thing to do. He credits Judge Barrett with persuading him to become a Republican.

If he did, Judge Barrett says now, he doesn't recall it. "I wouldn't care to argue with the Vice-President," he says with a quiet smile, "but it must have been a gradual thing. Certainly we talked politics in our office—Republican politics most of the time—and Ted often joined in. Certainly, I believed then, and I believe now, that there is more future for a young man in the minority party. And I felt Ted's views were more compatible with the Republican philosophy."

The Korean War came along. Ted Agnew was still in the Army Reserve and he was recalled to duty to be sent to that strange little police action. Their one-bedroom apartment was too crowded after Randy's birth and the family had moved to Baltimore County and into their first real home. It had a living room, kitchen, and four bedrooms—two unfinished on the second floor. Ted had somehow been able to make the payments.

When Ted was recalled it had to be sold. Judy and the children followed him, first to Fort George Meade, Maryland, and then to Fort Benning, George. After a year of going from training base to training base, he was released when the

Army found it had made a mistake: As a married man with a family, Ted Agnew could not be sent overseas.

Agnew found a newspaper ad seeking an assistant personnel director for Schreiber Brothers, a large Baltimore grocery chain. The salary was $100 a week. (Schreibers', they say in Maryland, refused to change with the times. It clung to its downtown locations, refused to move to the suburbs, and disappeared several years ago.)

There are many stories about Agnew's work at Schreibers', stories he dismisses with a smile. *The New York Times* says the title was a subterfuge, that he was a floor man who wore a white smock with his name tag on one side and "no tipping please" on the other. There are even stories he filled in as a food checker at the cash register.

The *New York Post,* in a series of articles on Agnew by reporter Jerry Tallmer, quotes Eugene Schreiber as saying Agnew was fired. He also quotes "another man in Baltimore" as saying it is a moot question whether Agnew was fired or quit.

Carl Gleitsmann, now a state employee, identified himself as that man in a letter to Agnew's office after he talked with Tallmer and "got the impression" Tallmer was trying to build a case against the Vice-President.

Gleitsmann said he worked for Schreiber Brothers for twenty years, and alongside Agnew when he worked there. He recalls Agnew as a "man of excellent character, well liked by employees and constantly going out of his way to help people." But he said Agnew had a "personality clash" with one of the four brothers, Martin Schreiber. Gleitsmann says this was not unusual because Martin Schreiber "was a most difficult person to work for and he fired many people."

He volunteered that Agnew had "a most happy relationship" with Negro workers and remembers him "going to bat" for a Negro who was in trouble to a small loan company.

His friends resent the stories about Agnew's job at Schreiber Brothers bitterly, though there is no reason why they should.

"They're trying to make him another Harry Truman," Sam Kimmel complains. "Not that Truman needs any defending, or that I'm the man to defend him."

Whatever else he did, Agnew functioned as an assistant personnel director at Schreibers' and he was a good one.

Once again this was one of his many lucky breaks. A good man usually makes his own breaks, anyhow.

Serving on Schreibers' board of directors at the time was Judge Herbert Moser. He came to know and like young Agnew. He got him a job with Karl Steinmann, a leading Baltimore attorney, now dead, but it didn't work out. To Agnew there seemed little prospect of advancement.

Judge Moser then found him a job with a research group working with the court of appeals rules committee. He opened a small office, and with his outside income to fall back on, managed to make $5,000 his first year.

One of his jobs at Schreibers' had been to negotiate with two Baltimore locals of the Amalgamated Meat Cutters and Butcher Workmen of North America, AFL-CIO. At first mistrustful of anyone connected with management, the meat cutters soon found Agnew fair and reasonable, a man with whom they could reach agreements. A bond of trust was forged.

Meanwhile, Governor McKeldin had appointed Michael Paul Smith to the circuit court in Baltimore County. Smith decided he was not cut out for the judiciary and resigned. McKeldin appointed Barrett to succeed him.

The suburbs beckoned. The Agnews moved first to Lutherville and then to Towson. Spiro T. Agnew had started on his way.

II

LABOR LAWYER

Spiro T. Agnew had found his life style.

A tall, well-built man, he had become an immaculate dresser, careful of his movements. His voice was soft, and rarely betrayed a carefully controlled temper. In public, he habitually wore what one friend described as a smile-grimace, which oddly had appeal and left others feeling they had shared a secret together.

He had become the kind of man who never takes off his tie in public and whose suits somehow defy wrinkling. He spoke in a monotone that in others would be deadening, and he seemed unable to end a sentence on an upbeat. Yet he was able to hold the attention of his listeners, whether a crowd or an individual.

He was, he liked to feel, a gentleman.

Towson is a town of some 25,000 people, two miles from the Baltimore city limits and six miles from the heart of the inner city.

It is as different from Baltimore city as day is from night.

Baltimore city and Baltimore County, by mutual consent, split away from each other before the Civil War.

Baltimore's business is industry; its waterfront is one of the nation's busiest.

Towson's is politics. Brad Jacobs, the *Sun's* able political commentator, refers to its atmosphere as one of "feuds, factions, and the artful stab by the light of the moon." It is no place for the weak or the squeamish.

But Towson is more. It is the home of Towson State College with its beautiful old-world campus and a growing student body of 5,000. (Agnew spoke at Towson State during the campaign and was heckled. The school prudently "disassociates" itself from the unpleasantries, an official says, because Agnew was not an "official invitee of the college.")

It is also the home of Goucher College, a renowned women's college, and a branch of Peabody Conservatory of Music.

It is a city of stately homes, peopled by many who have fled the inner city, side by side with jerry-built apartment complexes and multifamily dwellings.

It is a city to which one-way streets have recently come, to the annoyance of the old-timers.

It is also a city that takes pride in Towson Plaza, a modern shopping center with every convenience, but which is dominated, literally and figuratively, by its rambling two-story granite courthouse, built in 1855 at a cost of $30,000. (A modern, million-dollar county office building sits across the street, and it is from here that the county executive runs Baltimore County and its 625,000 citizens.)

It was to Towson that Spiro T. Agnew—he had acquired the nickname "Ted" in Judge Barrett's office in Baltimore but he was, and is still, Spiro to his wife—came in search of his fortune.

Towson was not impressed.

When Ted Agnew arrived, the ratio of Democrats to

Republicans on Baltimore County voter registration lists was 3.7 to 1. It had been as high as 4 to 1, as low as 3.5 to 1, but there was never a time the Democrats did not have a prohibitive majority.

Registration rolls then contained 158,000 Democrats and 41,000 Republicans.

Ted Agnew was one more Republican.

Most of the county's lawyers were Democrats, and most of the lucrative county legal business went to them. County lawyers practice not only before its courts—which, presumably, are blind to partisan distinctions—but also before zoning boards, liquor boards, appeals boards, and the county commissioners. It does not hurt a man's chance to be on the right side.

"When Ted Agnew and I arrived in Towson fifteen years ago," Sam Kimmel, Agnew's law partner recalls, "there weren't over two or three Republicans in the county—Tom Offutt, Scotty Moore (later to be Agnew's county attorney), and if there were any others their names escape me."

Occasionally, from the old courthouse, someone threw Spiro T. Agnew a bone. Usually it was a bone no one else wanted.

Court records disclose that in 1958, the county paid him a seventy-five-dollar fee for appearing in a sanity case.

For four years he fought the case of an eighteen-year-old boy charged with car theft and found to be a mentally defective delinquent—a legal status unique to Maryland—by his old friend Judge Barrett.

Despite their friendship, Agnew took Barrett's ruling to the state court of appeals. As a defective delinquent, a person— juvenile or adult—is adjudged incapable of defending himself and is committed to a state institution until that condition is corrected. Convicted felons despise and fear it.

Judge Barrett eventually was upheld. But he says now that Agnew "helped write new law, it was an extremely interesting case from the legal point of view, and he did well."

For these labors Agnew got $250—$150 in one payment, and $100 in another. That is hardly enough to support a family.

One case from those early days in Towson later came back to embarrass him.

Early in the 1960's, Lester L. Grogg, a dairy farmer, and Robert L. Kelly, an eighteen-year-old later found to be mentally deficient, were indicted for the murder of Mrs. Katie

Hoffheiser, an elderly woman living on a farm in what Baltimore Countians quaintly refer to even yet as "up country."

She had recognized Grogg, the testimony revealed, and on Grogg's command, Kelly had shot and killed her.

Agnew had been appointed to represent Grogg, another attorney to represent Kelly. The jury found that Kelly was completely under Grogg's influence and control. Grogg was convicted of first-degree murder and sentenced to life in prison. Kelly drew five years, all of which were suspended, and was placed on probation.

Grogg began a lengthy fight for his freedom. He filed a handwritten statement with the court in which he asserted: "I feel my attorney [Agnew] didn't do his best for me." He said he had told Agnew one member of the jury had lied when he said they were not acquainted, that the juror actually disliked him, but that Agnew had done nothing to remove the man from the panel.

Grogg filed appeal after appeal and all were denied. Then after Agnew became county executive, James A. Gede, an attorney operating out of offices at 24 Pennsylvania in Towson, where Agnew had practiced when he first came to town, took the case.

Gede went to the state court of appeals with a claim that Agnew had been "incompetent". Actually, Gede explains now, the only grounds on which the appeals court will hear a post-conviction matter is legal incompetency. He says it was a legal matter and in no way personal. Nonetheless, a charge that the third most important man in Maryland was incompetent in his own profession made headlines.

Agnew was on the stand for an hour at the state capitol at Annapolis, explaining in detail what he had done in the Grogg case. The judges believed him and the case was thrown out.

Later, while he was governor, the Grogg case came up again in federal court. Again the charge was made that Agnew was incompetent. Just as promptly the appeal was dismissed.

Grogg is still in prison.

But this flotsam and jetsam was not enough to maintain a household or to make Agnew a household word in Baltimore County.

"I knew he was around and he was an attorney," Frank

Strickland, editor of the *Towson Jeffersonian* recalls, "but I seldom thought about him. I assumed he was making a living, but I never inquired how".

The *Jeffersonian* is, as its name implies, a Democratic newspaper and a moneymaker many metropolitan dailies might envy. Appearing once a week—then on Friday, now on Thursday—it consists, on an average, of thirty-two to forty-eight pages; twenty to twenty-five of these pages consists almost entirely of legal advertising, the result of its close alliance with what was then and has since reverted to being the county's leading party. It never failed to publish an editorial on the eve of an election headlined: "Why We should Vote Democratic."

Spiro Agnew was making a living, and a good one. He had bought a $35,000 home in Towson's exclusive Chatterleigh section. He had begun to learn golf and later became president of his country club. The Agnews entertained frequently, but informally. Judy had become what one Washington society writer called "Main Street plump." To match her husband's six foot three, she added to her five foot four with high heels. She thought of herself as strictly a homebody.

Agnew was an excellent piano player and no gathering was without his contribution. His tastes in music ran to Lawrence Welk and Montevani.

"Ted and Judy were our dearest friends in Towson," Judge Barrett says. "He could improvise and arrange a tune. Let someone make a clever remark, and the first thing you knew, Ted had put it to music."

Ted became president of the Loch Raven Kiwanis and later the Loch Raven Inter-Community Association.

But it was in PTA (Parent-Teacher Association) work he shone. He first became president of the Loch Raven Elementary School PTA while his children attended that school. When they moved on to Rodgers Forge High School, he followed them. Again, he became president of its PTA.

"Ted never joined anything, including the PTA, that he didn't become president," Sam Kimmel recalls. "And when he was running things, you knew there was a PTA in town."

Agnew made his eloquence felt.

"Whatever we were discussing," another parent recalls, "Ted Agnew made you feel it was the compelling issue of our time and that its success or failure depended on you. It might be new equipment for the playground, or an increase in teachers' salaries. Ted Agnew got you involved."

Judy Agnew credits this activity with the start of her husband's political career. "It started with the PTA and just went on to other things," she says.

What Ted Agnew was doing, unknown to Democrats like Frank Strickland and others, was practicing labor law. Most of it was out of town.

His brief tenure as assistant personnel director at Schreiber Brothers—even though he may also have been a floorwalker— had aroused interest in him at the meat cutters' national headquarters. They were eager to obtain his services, and his quick grasp of labor law, for themselves.

Agnew found their offer attractive. He was also deeply interested in the meat cutters—many of whom ran the butcher counters in in the big chain markets—and felt their cause was a good one.

He became legal counsel to local 117 in Baltimore, and conducted its contract negotiations. He seemed always to bring the two sides together. There were no strikes.

Eventually, however, the international union decided to merge Baltimore's two locals into a single larger one, not only to save money but to be able to exercise more muscle.

"That," says Leon Schachter, the meat cutters international vice-president of the eastern seaboard and its Washington lobbyist, "left us with one lawyer too many."

Schachter says Agnew "wanted to stay on and I wanted him. I liked his work and I liked his views. I didn't see where we could find a better attorney or a more willing worker."

Schachter put Agnew on his staff in his Washington office at 100 Indiana Avenue NW, within the shadow of the nation's Captiol, and let the other lawyer represent the Baltimore local. It was a compromise that satisfied everyone.

Kimmel recalls that Agnew once took him to an office somewhere in Washington, an elaborate office with stenographers, secretaries, and even a law library. "This is where I work," he told his friend.

Schachter says the office was his, one he shared with Agnew. "Ted came and went as he chose," he said. "He worked for me, and he had complete freedom to use my office."

Agnew's association with the Amalgamated Meat Cutters and Butcher Workmen of North America, AFL-CIO, continued until he was elected Baltimore County executive in 1962. For what it was worth, the meat cutters supported him in that race against the entrenched Democratic machine.

"He did some great work, some really interesting work, for us," Schachter says. "I always sent an organizer along, but Ted Agnew was our legal brains. It was a good investment on our part."

After Agnew became Vice-President and was put in charge of the space program—one of the many top-echelon responsibilities Richard Nixon assigned him—he appointed Schachter to the eighteen-man Citizens' Task Force on Space. His old boss in the meat cutters union flew with the Vice-President in Air Force Two to Cape Kennedy for the blastoff of Apollo 11.

"Our job," he says of the task force, "is to decide what we do on the moon after we get there and stay for a while."

Schachter says one of Agnew's preoccupations about this time was the menhaden fishermen along Chesapeake Bay on both the Virginia and Maryland shores. Menhaden is a small fish, caught just off shore, ground and used for fish meal and chickenfeed.

"They'd never really been brought into the picture," Schachter says. "Agnew did a great job organizing them and getting them decent wages and working conditions."

Among the menhaden fishermen in meat cutters local 315 were those at Kilmarnock, Virginia.

There were 800 of them.

All were black.

Today, grizzled John Ball, president of local 315, veteran of almost forty years on the fishing boats, reminisces fondly about the time "Mr. Agnew worked for us."

"He got us the best contract we ever had," Ball says. "We wanted him to come down here and live, but I guess he had more important things to do."

The Negro boatmen thought so highly of Agnew they purchased a piece of waterfront property and offered to build him a home there.

Agnew was touched, but politely refused.

Thomas M. Kerrigan, of New York, management's attorney-negotiator in the menhaden fishermen's contract, also thought highly of the man on the other side of the table.

Kerrigan says he and Agnew "were and are good friends."

"I know that some of the meat cutters liked him a great

deal," he said. "That was particularly true on the East Coast. Some in the Midwest were less enthusiastic. But you can't please them all."

Agnew was frequently away from Towson for long periods of time on union business, hardly the thing a man with political ambitions in his home county would do if he could avoid it. Agnew couldn't avoid it. He had a living to make.

He negotiated a contract with the Richmond Packing Company of Richmond, Virginia, the first ever signed there.

He negotiated another at Front Royal, Virginia. He negotiated still another at Norfolk.

He was involved in negotiations for fishermen members of the meat cutters union in Tuckerton and Port Monmouth, New Jersey; Lewes, Delaware; and Amagansett, New York.

"The only strike we ever called," Sam Kimmel says, "was in Courtland, Virginia. My God, that was awful. The membership was black, and they'd never had a day's vacation in their lives. They could have Christmas Day off if they asked for it—without pay. Ted called a strike in there, but we lost it. We just couldn't buck management, and the blacks had to go back to work on the company's terms. It was sickening. Ted and I cried over it."

Agnew's association with the union continued even after he had been elected county executive. When, after three years as head man in Baltimore County, he decided to run for governor as a Republican, he sought out his old boss, Leon Schachter.

The two were accustomed to plain talk.

Agnew asked for the union's support in the Republican primary and got it. He hardly needed it. He was more interested in the general election.

On the Democratic side, organized labor was strongly behind Carleton Sickles, long a labor favorite, a Kennedyesque liberal, representing a Washington suburban district in Congress for his second term.

Agnew asked who the meat cutters would support if it were Sickles against Agnew.

Schachter said they would go for Sickles.

Agnew nodded.

He asked what would happen if George Mahoney, making his seventh bid for high state office, were the Democratic nominee.

"My God," Schachter said, "we could never go for Mahoney. We'll be behind you a thousand percent."

And so, it turned out, they were.

But that is getting ahead of our story. Meanwhile, Agnew had become interested in the Republican post on the county zoning board of appeals. Under Maryland law, one member of the three-man board must come from the opposition party.

Few things arouse the passions in suburban America that zoning does. There is a never-ending clash between developers and conservationists, traditionalists and modernists. Millions of dollars are involved, and some builders are not averse to spreading them around, particularly if they will influence the votes of those who decide what they can or cannot do.

Every board meeting is bedlam, with opposing sides shouting at one another, and accusations of dishonesty, malfeasance, and wrongdoing are commonplace.

"I can't understand why anyone would want it," Edward Hardesty, who succeeded Agnew on the zoning board and has held the job for eight years, says. "You live in a goldfish bowl. You've got to be so careful who you're seen with, who you have a drink with, even who gives you a cigar. It's hardly worth it."

Agnew wanted it. And the Democratic county council was eventually persuaded to give it to him. That was in 1958.

In return for being rescued from political limbo, the Republican member of the Baltimore county board of zoning appeals was expected to remain dutifully quiet. All had.

But that was not Ted Agnew's way.

At his first meeting he demanded that the Baltimore County state's attorney—a party stalwart—be censored for failing to carry out a board order.

Democratic leaders who had voted for his appointment were aghast.

Not too discreetly, they suggested his resignation.

Agnew refused.

Still later, he shocked the board by demanding that it stop requiring cash deposits from those appealing its decisions to the court. This was traditional in Baltimore County; no one had ever questioned the practice. It wasn't much—two dollars—but Agnew argued it impinged on a citizen's right.

In meeting after meeting, Agnew asked questions the

majority felt should not be asked, wrote opinions that aired matters best left on the back burner, cast an embarrassing minority vote.

When he came up for reappointment, the Democrats were determined to drop this renegade.

On the night appointed, the council chamber was jammed. Some councilmen charged they were pressured to vote for Agnew. Members of civic groups, attorneys, and the Citizens Planning and Housing Association were present. They waved banners. They shouted. They stamped their feet.

In Baltimore County, it was an unprecedented demonstration.

The council voted 5 to 2, to oust their maverick. A "safe" Republican was picked to succeed him. Agnew's supporters tramped angrily from the County Office Building, vowing vengeance.

It was another of those lucky breaks that have characterized Spiro Agnew's career. His name was now a household word in Baltimore County.

He had his issue.

He was moving on his way.

III

THE BREAKTHROUGH

Baltimore County was a Democratic fiefdom. Its laird was Michael Birmingham. Not since 1885 had it known anything but Democratic party rule. And not, in recent times, had anyone but Michael Birmingham made the political decisions that affected it and its people.

Wealthy, generous, warmhearted, Michael Birmingham honestly regarded Baltimore County as his own. He bestowed, or withheld, favors as he felt right. He smiled on the worthy and scowled at the disinherited. He had instant entree at the statehouse, no matter who was governor, for he could guarantee substantial majorities from his people, which often meant the difference between victory and defeat.

Some metropolitian dailies—as, for example, *The New York Times*—have referred to his "corrupt" rule. People in

Towson feel differently. Even those who opposed him politically speak well of him—he is since deceased—as a man.

"He did a lot for this county," they say, or "He gave more than he took ... he was honest ... we wouldn't be where we are today without him. ..."

They may compare him to Boss Frank Hague of Jersey City, or Tom Pendergast of Kansas City. But they are careful to say there is no blot on his record, and people loved him.

It was just that—although he could not have known it—Michael Birmingham's time had come. He had seen his fiefdom grow from a rural paradise to a suburban metropolis. He had seen industry replace barns and dairy farms, superhighways the country roads, and had watched towering skyscrapers reach into the sky.

Michael Birmingham had been around too long.

Birmingham was chairman of the board of county commissioners when Spiro Agnew moved to Towson. If Birmingham acknowledged the newcomer's presence at all, it was to take his hand and bid him welcome. As a Republican, Agnew could expect no favors, and he got none. Mike Birmingham continued to dispense favors in his own style.

As a blow in the direction of change—and even Michael Birmingham could feel its cold wind on his neck—the state had decided to abolish the county commission form of government in Baltimore County and elect a county executive. It was the popular thing to do. Presumably, or so the brochures said, it automatically meant good, clean government—instant Utopia.

Mike Birmingham went along. He felt he knew when to fight and when to give in gracefully. As a concession to him, the law said that the first county executive would be the then sitting commission chairman.

That man, of course, was Michael Birmingham.

Birmingham's close friend and fellow commissioner was another businessman, Christian H. Kahl. Kahl had labored long and well in the party's political vineyards. He had delivered substantial majorities from his precincts to both county and state tickets. If he resented playing second fiddle to his old and dear friend he never betrayed it. The two seemed inseparable.

Mike Birmingham was not a greedy man. After his term—which gave him the distinction of being the first county executive—he decided to let old Chris have a go at it. He was sure it would mean no change of pace, no shift in the regular order of county business. Mike was accustomed to running things from the wings. And Kahl deserved the honor. Kahl was elected in 1958. For a while he behaved as expected. But as time went on he began making appointments without consulting his old friend, appointments Michael Birmingham definitely did not approve. The seven-man Baltimore Council, very much under Birmingham's control, began turning them back.

This should have been warning enough, but it only made a man like Chris Kahl more stubborn. He began to speak of Mike Birmingham in an unfriendly way, as a dictator and a tyrant. Democrats, accustomed to serving one master, were confused. As the breach widened they were forced to choose. The faithful were unaccustomed to choice. Their decisions had always been made for them.

One of the decisions Kahl made was to appoint an upstart, Spiro T. Agnew, only a few years out of the city, to the board of zoning appeals. Agnew had behaved—as far as Birmingham Democrats were concerned—in an abominable fashion. He had muddied waters best left calm; he had offended Michael Birmingham deeply.

Kahl felt he could not really be blamed. Judge Barrett— now presiding circuit judge—had introduced Agnew to Congressman James Devereaux, who represented Baltimore County in Washington. Agnew had worked hard in Devereaux's last two campaigns. A retired Marine brigadier general, hero of Wake Island, where, he loudly insists, he did *not* say: "Send us more Japs" (some Marine public information officer in Washington did, however, and attributed it to him), Devereaux, even though a Republican, pulled considerable political weight in Baltimore County, perhaps second only to Michael Birmingham.

Devereaux had served eight years in Congress, giving up his seat to run as his party's sacrificial lamb against J. Millard Tawes, an Eastern Shore banker, in the last gubernatorial election. It was in response to Devereaux that Kahl agreed to ask the council to approve Agnew. Kahl respected Devereaux's obvious political muscle, but he also admired the old general as a patriot.

When the board of zoning appeals was abolished and a zoning commissioner and deputy were created to replace it, the council twice rejected Kahl's appointments. They were, it felt, too anti-Birmingham. At least they could not be counted on to be pro-Birmingham. And by this time anything Kahl did was suspect anyhow.

Kahl announced he would seek reelection in 1962. Birmingham promptly announced he would oppose him.

For Baltimore County, it was an unprecedented situation.

Most of the top county party leaders lined up behind Birmingham. Kahl had his courthouse patronage, or what was left of it.

Up and down the county the two old men campaigned, their claws unsheathed, their fangs bared. Birmingham regarded Kahl as an ingrate and said so. Kahl said Birmingham was a tyrant, and deserved a tyrant's fate. It was an angry, heartbreaking fight, particularly to the faithful who had loved and served both men.

It tore the Democratic party apart.

Birmingham's forces lined up with Tawes's administration. Many of his friends say that was his undoing. He felt—rightly, as far as the primary was concerned—it guaranteed his election. After that, they say, he waged a lackluster campaign.

Kahl, the underdog, continued on the attack, ripping, tearing, charging.

The breach was irreparable.

When the votes were counted, Birmingham had won, but by too narrow a margin. He had 37,160 votes, Kahl had 34,660.

This, of course, made headlines in the *Towson Jeffersonian*. (There is now another newspaper in town, the *Towson Times*, but E. Scott Moore, Agnew's old county attorney, says "It's only been here a short time, we don't know much about it." The *Times* is three years old.)

The *Jeffersonian* carried another, smaller, story that day.

"Spiro T. Agnew, Towson attorney," it reported, "is the sole Republican candidate for county executive. Having no opposition, he was not required to run in the primary."

By way of further explanation, lest its readers be confused, it added: "Mr. Agnew lives at 1830 Aberdeen Road, Towson, with his wife and four children."

Christian Kahl reported he had spent $102,415.31 on the campaign. Michael Birmingham had spent $72,240.42. Spiro T. Agnew had spent nothing.

The campaign resumed, this time between Birmingham and Agnew. Again, it was an unprecedented situation. Not, in recent memory, had a Republican made a serious bid for Baltimore County office. Ted Agnew was dead serious.

Agnew was everywhere. He rallied the civic associations behind him, called on his coworkers in the Loch Raven and Rodgers Forge PTA, revived the zoning scandals, charged the Democratic machine was moribund and incapable of change. His campaign style, his oratory, defying all the rules, caught hold as it would in later campaigns. No one could explain why. He stood rooted to the rostrum. His gestures were jerky. He seldom raised his voice.

Yet he came through.

Perhaps tired by the emotional break with his old friend, Birmingham waged another lackluster campaign. He obviously had no serious doubts about winning; he always had. But there were times, he told friends, when he wondered if he wanted too.

When the votes were counted on November 8, 1962, Agnew had won a resounding victory, 78,487 votes to Birmingham's 60,993.

"They voted against Birmingham, not only for Agnew," Frank Strickland, editor of the *Jeffersonian,* says. Nevertheless, Agnew was to become Baltimore County's first major Republican officeholder in seventy-seven years.

If Agnew had achieved his goal, he had not been able to carry his ticket with him. He succeeded in electing one Republican to the seven-man council. Two others went to the state legislature. But the majorities rested firmly in the control of the Democrats. Sam Kimmel, Agnew's law partner, ran for a seat in the assembly and lost.

The *Jeffersonian* had run its customary editorial—"Why We Should Vote Democratic"—on the the eve of the election. Yet it was a bit more generous with Agnew than it had been with others. After he won the Republican nomination without opposition he was identified merely as a Towson attorney. Now he became "Towson attorney, law professor and former member of the board of zoning appeals." Agnew had taught torts one night a week for two semesters at Baltimore Law University. He was an instructor.

Birmingham and Kahl both came forward with the expected congratulatory messages and promises of support. Baltimore County, Birmingham said, was bigger than either political party. Kahl echoed that, and—perhaps to rub salt in his old friend's wounds—offered to help Agnew during the transition.

The honeymoon lasted one week.

Among the second-echelon Democrats who had broken ranks and supported Agnew was Ed Hardesty. Hardesty was one of Agnew's law partners. Kahl had appointed him an assistant state's attorney. In that postion he had been assigned to zoning cases. This in effect, made him Agnew's county lawyer.

At the council's first meeting, Agnew offered Hardesty's name as deputy zoning director, a post for which the council had rejected Kahl's last two nominations.

The Democratic-controlled council was determined to punish Hardesty's apostasy in supporting Agnew. The meeting was long, the debate bitter. In the end, Hardesty was rejected by a vote of 5 to 2. Among those voting for him was Dale Anderson, a Democratic councilman who was to succeed Agnew as county executive.

Agnew's reaction was one the nation had come to expect. He was coldly furious.

"Obviously," he said after the meeting, "the interests of the council were directed at Mr. Hardesty's political alignments and not at his ability or experience. The council's action was hasty, ill-considered, and spearheaded by one of its weakest members."

Agnew was determined to have Hardesty in his official family, specifically as his zoning man. And—four months after it had rejected him—in May the county council reversed itself and approved Hardesty's nominations by a vote of 5 to 2.

Agnew's idolators like to claim he "wore them down," that he was so insistent on Hardesty's confirmation they gave up and let him have his man.

Politics, at the county level, doesn't work that way.

Hardesty has a slightly different version.

"He staked his prestige on me," Hardesty says with extreme candor. "Everything hinged on my being confirmed. It was strictly a political deal. It would have to be in a county like Baltimore with its Democratic majority. Ted is a practical politician. Certain prominent Democrats were protected in their jobs, and, in return, I was confirmed. It was as simple as that."

But Hardesty insists it was personal friendship, rather than political advantage, that made Agnew fight for him.

"It was a personal thing," he says. "I had practiced before the zoning board, and Ted liked my style. I was in his law office. He always knew that I was a Democrat, and he never put any pressure on me to change. That is like him. If he takes a liking to you, he's for you all the way. I think you'll find that many of his closest friends are Democrats. He was furious when I was rejected, and Ted Agnew furious is a sight to behold. He wouldn't be satisfied until I got the job."

Surprisingly, all his other appointments were confirmed, among them General Devereaux, retired from Congress after his defeat by Governor Tawes, to be county safety commissioner. It was a fitting post for the hero of Wake Island. In effect, it made him county police chief.

Agnew's record as county executive was a progressive one, particularly for a county as steeped in conservatism as Baltimore County. He proposed a county income tax. He forced through a civil-rights program, including a public accommodations section, the first local civil-rights program south of the Mason-Dixon line. He proposed, and got, a public kindergarten—"I'll come up with the money somehow"—used principally by Negro women who worked for a living.

His worst—and only major—defeat came on the issue of urban renewal. Baltimore County just wouldn't swallow that.

In 1964, Agnew included in a proposed $31 million county bond issue one for $3.8 mission to match federal funds that would initiate urban renewal in East Towson, a rundown Negro section, and along York Road, a retail district that had seen its best days.

He threw himself into the fight.

"Private enterprise, in spite of good intentions, cannot even begin to undertake a rejuvenation of such proportions," he insisted.

"He was very intense about urban renewal," Strickland recalls. "As a newspaper, we played it straight; we were getting advertisement from both sides. We often ran two pages of letters to the editor, the most violently opposed. But if the paper kept quiet, Ted knew where I stood. I was against it. I thought it was a mistake. Baltimore County wasn't ready for it. What people really objected to was bringing federal money into our county. They felt that would be just the first step.

"I was out with him one night. Jim Devereaux was in the party. I don't remember what it was—it was some little thing—but Ted blew up. He raised hell. He was furious. I was his target, but it was only because he was so keyed up about the bond issue. We never mentioned it again."

Agnew put his old mentor, General Devereaux, out front in the fight. It must have been a galling experience for the former congressman, whose every vote in the House of Representatives for eight years had been against such expenditures. If he had still been in Washington, urban renewal would have been dirty words.

But he performed loyally. Reminding Baltimore County of his record, he staunchly insisted that the urban-renewal plans of his friend Ted Agnew were "progressive and vitally needed."

He could have saved his breath. On November 2, 1964, Baltimore County rejected urban renewal by a vote of 93,446 to 58,988. To make their point even more explicit, every other bond issue in the $31-million offering was approved.

Typically, Agnew refused to admit he had been licked.

Urban renewal, he said, is inevitable. He and the county council, he said, would have to find other monies to do the things the voters had told him he could not do.

He left to become governor before he could make good on that.

Agnew's intensity in one-time rural Baltimore County disturbed some, including his friends. He was early on the job, late to leave. He tackled each problem as if the fate of mankind depended on its immediate solution.

That was not the Baltimore County way. Its politics were deadly duels, but daily operations of a political job, once secured, were more relaxed. Ted Agnew's pace upset the whole courthouse.

His only relaxation was attending the Baltimore Colts football games during the National Football League season. He and Judge Barrett had owned three season tickets each to the Colts' games since the team had come into the NFL. They were both rabid Colt fans who never missed a game. During his campaign for the Vice-Presidency Agnew told reporters at Chicago he had missed his first Colt game, "and that hurts."

Their seats—six in a row—were on the 20-yard line. Both men insisted they were vastly to be preferred over seats on the 50-yard line. Agnew's fierce loyalties were concentrated on the Colts; he could name every player, and knew as much as there was to know about him. Judge Barrett's devotion to the Colts was, and is, shared by his love of the Baltimore Orioles. Agnew was "only moderately" an Oriole fan.

Agnew continued to sit on the 20-yard line even after he became governor. He tried it once after his election as Vice-President. There wasn't enough room. Nearby ticketholders had to be ejected—over their loud complaints—to make room for the Secret Service. Since then, Agnew has sat in the press box.

He began to learn golf.

"He'd call me up and ask, 'How about nine tomorrow morning?'," Frank Strickland recalls. "Of course, we never played nine; it was always eighteen. I'm an average weekend golfer; he was just learning. I usually won, but he got better all the time. As far as I know, that was the only time he ever took away from the job at the courthouse."

Throughout 1965, Agnew kept his eye on the statehouse in Annapolis. It was obvious the Democratic party was headed for a dogfight. George Mahoney, a wealthy road contractor, was determined to make another try. Six times he had run either for governor or United States senator. When he was able, as he sometimes was, to get the Democratic nomination, he could never win in the general election.

Congressman Carleton Sickles was itching to run.

So was Maryland State Attorney General Tom Finan (now associate judge of the court of appeals and out of politics).

Conditions looked right. Agnew had established a reputation as a fighter for progressive causes. Liberals all over the state liked his record. He would make a particularly strong race if Mahoney were nominated. The only way to anticipate that was to secure the Republican nomination.

On April 21, 1966, he filed. He was accompanied to the statehouse by his wife and fifteen of his friends, including former Governor Theodore McKeldin; Representative Rodgers C. B. Morton (R.-Md.), now GOP National Chairman; and former U.S. Senator John Marshall Butler. Representative Charles Mac Mathias (R.-Md.), soon to become a United States senator, sent word he would have come but he was in the hospital.

Agnew's course was set.
He was definitely on his way.

IV

ANNAPOLIS

Spiro T. Agnew's political fate hung perilously in the balance throughout the night of September 13, 1966, and into the early morning.

His own Republican gubernatorial nomination had been nailed down soon after the polls closed. No one expected differently. A covey of unknowns—an engineer, a school-teacher, a perennial candidate—picked up a vote here, another there. Agnew's totals spiraled into the thousands. They might as well not have counted them.

But the Free State of Maryland has three registered Dem-ocrats for every one Republican, and since the turn of this century had had but three Republican governors. Ted Agnew's chances of becoming the fourth depended—he and his backers were absolutely sure—upon George Mahoney's getting the Democratic nomination.

A paving contractor and multimillionaire before he was forty, youngest of the eleven children of a Baltimore police-man, tough, quick-tempered, sentimental, Mahoney was making his seventh bid for election in a statewide race.

Back in 1940 a former governor, the late Herbert O'Con-er, had named him a member, then chairman, of the state racing commission. Mahoney won the plaudits of FBI Direc-tor J. Edgar Hoover with his charges that Maryland racing was crooked, that horses were doped, and "the little guy" the two-dollar bettor, was being taken to the cleaners.

O'Conor's successor, the late William Preston Lane, Jr., first fired him, then, as a gesture of appeasement, made Mahoney Democratic national committeeman. Mahoney was not to be appeased. The list of those he has since opposed— Lane, the late Representative Lansdale G. Sasscer, University of Maryland President H. C. Byrd, the late U.S. Senator Millard E. Tydings, Sickles, Finan, Governor Tawes—reads like a Who's Who of Maryland politics.

In his battle with Tydings, Mahoney had promised the voters: "If you don't want me, I won't come back and bother you anymore; I won't impose on you again." It was a promise he could not keep. George Mahoney honestly believes he has something people of Maryland need, and will not take "no" for an answer until he has put it to the test.

The Democratic primary campaign had been a nasty one. Mahoney had filed early. So had Representative Carleton Sickles, darling of the liberals. On their heels came Tom Finan, state attorney general, standard-bearer of the party machine headed by Governor Tawes. Each had their slates for state comptroller and attorney general. There were others in the race—unknown men—but these three, Mahoney, Sickles, and Finan, were the ones who mattered.

Sickles and Finan made the mistake of ignoring Mahoney. Sickles campaigned against Finan. Finan campaigned against Sickles. Only Governor Tawes over in the statehouse in Annapolis took an occasional swipe at the man who had so tormented him four years earlier.

Sickles accused Finan of a conflict of interest. Finan lashed back that Sickles was "the captive of organized labor." Sickles said the Tawes administration, of which Finan was a part, had let the state's oyster beds go to pot. Finan said Sickles had been a part-time congressman, more interested in his labor clients than the people he had been elected to represent.

Mahoney's slogan was "Your Home Is Your Castle— Protect It." Most Baltimoreans were convinced they knew what that meant. If they were not sure, Mahoney came out flatly against open housing. He said he would veto any civil-rights legislation, including open housing, that the general assembly might pass. But he denied that he was a racist.

"Look," he said, "I don't care if you're a white man or Chinaman or a Negro. Suppose someone wants to rent your house and he has fifteen children and ten dogs. You turn him down. You could be fined or go to jail if you say 'No.' I'll fight a law like that to my last breath."

In the row houses with their white stepes—a Baltimore tradition—the workingmen's families nodded solemn approval. In the neighborhood bars they loved him. Sickles and Finan caught on too late.

Ted Agnew sat before his TV set watching the returns,

returns that would seal his fate although he was not directly involved.

From the start, it was close.

With 90 percent of the vote in, shortly after midnight, Congressman Sickles held a slight lead—125,313 votes to 124,050 for Mahoney. Finan was close behind with 116,218.

It was four A.M. before the unofficial results from all the State's precincts were in. Ironically, it was Ted Agnew's own Baltimore County that clinched the results. Mahoney also lives in Baltimore County. A breakdown in the voting machines had delayed reporting its figures until very late.

Mahoney had 144,174 votes, Sickles had 141,337, and Finan had 131,270.

Mahoney was the Democratic nominee with 30 percent of the vote. There is no provision for a runoff in Maryland.

Agnew was elated. To no one's surprise he confessed he was "gratified" Mahoney had won. He had figured him all along as the easiest man to beat. This was an understatement. Already Maryland Republicans were stripping down for a serious campaign. Before it was over Agnew would spend almost $400,000, an unparalled campaign chest for the state's Republicans.

There were still a few tense moments. Absentee ballots were still to be counted, and at one time they cut Mahoney's lead to 934 votes. Agnew fretted while Sickles talked about a recount. Eventually Mahoney's victory margin was established at 1,034 votes—146,152 to 145,118. Finan trailed with 133,149.

As in Baltimore County in 1962, the Democratic party was split. Democrats-for-Agnew clubs sprang up all over the state. Former Secretary of State Dean Acheson, living in Montgomery County just outside Washington, threw his support to Agnew. Sickles said he could not endorse the man who had beaten him, that obviously he could not ask others to vote for a man he wasn't sure would get his vote. Senator Joseph D. Tydings, who had supported Sickles, said had "not yet determined the extent of my involvement, if any, in support of Mr. Mahoney." Royce Hanson, the Democratic candidate for Congress in Maryland's Tenth Congressional District, withheld his support. A Baltimore banker who had been finance chairman for both Presidents Kennedy and Johnson called for Mahoney's defeat—and Agnew's election.

The campaign between Agnew and Mahoney began in

earnest. As in the Democratic primary, there were three candidates. Hyman A. Pressman, Baltimore city comptroller, had entered as an Independent.

Mahoney kicked it off by calling Agnew a "slob." In fact, he called the immaculate clotheshorse from the Baltimore suburbs a "big slob." Agnew, according to press reports, chuckled.

Agnew—with Pressman joining him—challenged Mahoney to a televised debate. Mahoney retorted he "wouldn't dare go on television with those two nuts." He had good reason. Agnew's speaking style, always top-rate, had steadily improved. He had become master of first the gentle stab, then, later, the piercing one. Pressman, a maverick, adopted the style of whirling dervish on TV. Mahoney was not even a fair public speaker. He was awful. He stumbled through prepared speeches and, on his own, butchered the language, oftentimes losing his temper and shouting.

His first press conference after winning the Democratic nomination degenerated into a wild, at times raucous, question-and-answer period with reporters, which did nothing to heal the rift in the party. Among other things Mahoney lashed out at the "element in the party [which tried] to label me a racist and a bigot."

Agnew was pleased. He let Mahoney talk on. He took the high road.

Agnew carried his own brand of blunt honesty into the campaign. Addressing an insurance workers union meeting in Prince George County, he refused to give snap answers.

"There are ten different avenues to take on some of these problems, and I am not going to stand here and tailor one just to get your vote."

Asked by a commuter, "What about new roads to get us into Washington?" he said: "New roads and superhighways are not the answer. We must have mass transit. Los Angeles has superhighways wherever you look, but they not only haven't solved the problem, but have taken billions of dollars of property off the tax rolls and put the city in a financial bind."

Periodically, Mahoney tried to win back dissident Democrats. But Prince Georges County, Sickles' home county, would merely "recognize," not endorse him. He met with Montgomery County precinct chairmen to explain himself—and was met by total silence. Party leaders in that wealthy, liberal Washington suburb made it plain he'd get no financial support from them.

Agnew charged Mahoney had mimicked a Negro in a speech before Baltimore realtors. He said Mahoney was a bigot. Mahoney came right back charging that Agnew was guilty of racism "in its rawest form."

Why? Because, Mahoney said, Agnew had promised to appoint Negroes to public office if elected. He said Agnew had spoken to crowds at predominantly Negro Morgan State College and to other Negro groups. Mahoney branded these "outright appeals to Negroes to base their votes on the color of their skins."

Later, after he became Governor and Vice-President, Agnew would have to fight charges that he was anti-Negro.

Mahoney was furious when a man identifying himself as Xavier Edwards, and claiming to be the imperial wizard of the Maryland Ku Klux Klan, endorsed him. He said Agnew had put him up to it. He promptly rejected the Klan offer.

The campaign got meaner.

Agnew charged that he had been offered $200,000 by the slot-machine interests if he would agree not to veto legislation extending their legality. Slots had been an issue in Maryland for years, and the legislature finally had voted to outlaw them in counties where they were legal. It gave them a five-year grace period to phase out. Some Maryland counties depended upon slots almost entirely. Now the grace period was ending and there was a move afoot to give them more time.

Agnew said he would not even talk to "them." He said the offer came to him third or fourth hand, that those who controlled the machines were too smart to approach him directly.

Mahoney charged that his life had been threatened. He canceled a breakfast appearance in Calvert County and went into seclusion with his aids and karate expert Ed Helms, the personal bodyguard the Baltimore police had assigned him. But by nightfall he was back—telling an American Legion audience in LaPlata that a "Republican governor could kill you—I don't mean that literally—in the halls of Annapolis."

Someone set fire to an automobile owned by one of Mahoney's aides, and a mysterious caller told him "Mahoney's next." Agnew was shocked and distressed that a man, regardless of viewpoint, cannot seek public office without suffering such indignities."

It was October 13 before Agnew and Pressman were able to meet with Mahoney. He had sent aides to all other meetings. It was a meeting on traffic safety sponsored by the state medical and chirurgical faculty and the Maryland chapter of the American College of Suregons.

Pressman called attention to the fact that this "is the first time anyone has seen the three candidates on the same platform." Agnew said he "wanted to commend Mr. Mahoney for this first, hesitant step into the political arena." Mahoney ignored them. He spoke and left.

Agnew had attended a luncheon in New York given him by fellow Americans of Greek ancestry. He said later they had contributed about $3,500 to his campaign fund.

Mahoney professed to see something negative in this. He told a suburban rally: "The Greeks in New York and some of the worst characters in the world sit around together. If Agnew gets nasty, I'll be compelled to talk about it."

Several times thereafter he made mysterious references to something he "had on" Agnew and might "have to tell." He kept his secret.

Mahoney never succeeded in bringing his party together. As the campaign progressed, Agnew became more and more confident he would be the winner.

Tawes and Finan were giving the Mahoney ticket their nominal support. Agnew produced a four-year-old statement by Tawes describing Mahoney as "unfit for public office."

"Nothing has happened since to make Mr. Mahoney any more fit," he said.

The *Baltimore Sun* endorsed Agnew in a backhanded way. Mahoney, it said editorially, "is totally unfit to run this state."

As the voting neared, Agnew stepped up his attacks. He accused Mahoney of "basing his campaign on a protest against open housing" and ignoring other major issues facing the state. He was particularly incensed by a handbill attempting to relate Mahoney's candidacy to the assassination of President Kennedy. Pictures of Mahoney and Kennedy were prominently displayed. Next to Kennedy's picture was this message: "This man was a victim of hate." Next to Mahoney's: "Our next governor's life has been threatened because of his courageous defense of your home." Agnew replied that "Kennedy stood for all the things Mahoney is against. I am reminded of the words of the little Irish lawyer [Joseph N. Welch] during the McCarthy hearings: 'Sir, have you no sense of decency?' "

Mahoney spent the night before the election in a confrontation with Agnew's old friends in local 117 of the meat cutters union. Four years before the local had supported him against Tawes. Now it was for Agnew.

With Mahoney glaring, local Secretary Jerry Menapace told members, including Negroes, that "the people who have hooked onto Mahoney's coattails have been our enemies all our lives. . . . The image he has created is anti-Negro, anti-union, anti-Catholic." Mahoney said Menapace "isn't telling the truth. . . . You supported me four years ago, I don't know what's come over you!"

On Election Day, Agnew voted, then played golf. That night the Agnew family retired to a Baltimore hotel suite to await the returns. For the children it was a disappointment. They had visualized something more exciting; instead, "We just sat in a room and looked at a TV set." Ten-year-old Kim was more upset with her father. When he had decided to run for governor, Agnew, as was his custom, called a family conference and asked for a vote. It was unanimous, but Kim's vote was conditional. He could run, but he must not win. She did not want to leave her friends in Towson.

It wasn't even close. Spiro Agnew got approximately 50 percent of the vote, Mahoney 40 percent, and Pressman 10 percent. The totals were: Agnew, 452,838; Mahoney, 370,-929; and Pressman, 89,567 votes.

Mahoney, as had been expected, ran strongly in the white working-class districts of Baltimore and in the Baltimore suburbs where Ted Agnew had gotten his start. But he lost the city of Baltimore as a whole with its large Negro vote.

Agnew ran strongest in the white liberal suburbs of Washington, as well as in the traditionally Republican mountain country in the western part of the state.

The "Dixie belt" counties on the Eastern Shore of Chesapeake Bay—there had been racial disturbances in Cambridge—supported Mahoney, but not as overwhelmingly as some experts had predicted. One reason apparently was that Mahoney is a devout Catholic, and there was some anti-Catholic feeling in that region.

Agnew was elected, but Democratic candidates for state

comptroller and attorney general on Mahoney's ticket won easily.

Mahoney was predictable in conceding defeat. Sixty-four years old, and looking it, choking back tears, he acknowledged that his seventh bid for high office had been turned back. But he wouldn't say he would not run again.

"How can a man know what's ahead?" he asked. "You can't know."

The next few weeks were hectic ones, particularly for Judy Agnew. They had sold the ten-room house she had known as home in Chatterleigh and she was depressed by the knowledge that, for the first time since she had moved to Towson, she hadn't a house she could call her own.

She toured the historic governor's mansion in Annapolis and found it "charming," but secretly made notes of changes she would make.

Kim was disconsolate at leaving Towson, but Susan, nineteen, and Randy twenty, were delighted with Annapolis. They said the mansion would be a great place for a party. Sue found the servants "hard to get used to" and Randy was afraid they'd "always have to be on guard . . . we won't know who is visiting." But overall, they were pleased.

Randy was soon to go into the service, despite the fact that he was married and would soon be a father. (Agnew would name his chartered plane for the baby when he campaigned for the Vice Presidency.) He wound up with the Seabees in Vietnam, and was there near Danang when his father was nominated for the second highest post in the nation.

Judy Agnew grieved while he was gone for their daughter-in-law, who wanted Randy home for the birth of their first child. It was a reminder of her loneliness when Pamela, now twenty-three years old and about to be married, was born during World War II.

Spiro T. Agnew was inaugurated governor of the Free State of Maryland on January 25, 1967. Judge Hall Hammond of the state court of appeals administered the oath. His inaugural address cribbed a bit and was devoted to "the pursuit of excellence." Maryland, he said, "must join the quest for equality and decency that these times demand. . . .

"We have lived with old laws too long and resisted new ideas too easily," he said. "Without change, immediate and positive change, we will become merely the custodians of a static state."

He called for fiscal reform, an attack on air and water pollution, renewal of decaying urban areas, and new solutions for crime problems.

"It has become all too obvious that the cost of failure far exceeds the price of progress," he said.

Democrates, accustomed to running the state, were not impressed. They still controlled both houses of the general assembly.

"My God, would you believe it," cracked State Senator Roy Slaten, a Baltimore County Democrat, "the man's actually endorsed excellence!"

Some of their laughter soon subsided. Three months later the *Baltimore Sun* described the state's new governor as "a quietly decisive executive who has grown in self-assurance." Later, after two years in office, the *Sun*'s astute political columnist, Brad Jacobs, was to write:

"The Agnew imprint has become clear.

"He is not, as Governor [J. Millard] Tawes, a canny consensus seeker.

"He is not a [Governor Theodore R.] McKeldin-like exotic, no thrusting commander of the order of Governor [William Preston] Lane.

"Mr. Agnew represents a new generation of politician, a generation coolly alert to the realities of political power, but less interested in power itself than in what power can do."

Agnew realized that as a minority governor he must quickly establish himself as a man ready to make decisions.

He did not hesitate to be unpopular. Agnew had campaigned on the necessity for tax reform, which included a graduated income tax hike of two to five percent. Democratic Governor Tawes had asked for one, but it had failed by two votes, largely because Tawes did not exert himself. At the Montgomery County Fair outside Washington, Agnew was asked by a heckler: "When're you going to lower our taxes?" His reply was, "I'm sorry I can't. I can't see any way to finance the state without raising them."

Working with the Democratic controlled state legislature, he got his tax hike. He smiled wryly as anguished howls went up all over Maryland. Legislators who had sent the measure to his desk stayed away in droves. He was unable to give away a single souvenir pen used in signing it.

But he also suspended embattled State Correction Commissioner Vernon L. Pepersack, who presided over a scandal-ridden prison system, and order a cleanup. This move was widely applauded around the state. He eased out the state roads commission chairman and fired the holdover public improvements director. He named Dr. Gilbert Ware of the United States Civil Rights Commission, a respected Princeton man, to his personal staff. Among his duties was the supervision of state welfare programs.

Yet, to be fair, many Democrats held onto the job they had under Tawes, as Democrats did in Baltimore County when he had been county executive. He came to an accommodation with state house Speaker Marvin Mandel, the Democrat who was to succeed him as governor when he became Vice-President. The *Baltimore Sun* remarked that Governor Agnew had been "forced to strike politically expensive bargains to achieve his ends." He could hardly do otherwise.

Occasionally, there were political clashes between Governor Agnew and Attorney General Francis Burch and between Agnew and Comptroller Louis Goldstein, the number-one and number-two men in the state government. Both were Democrats.

Less than a week after he was sworn in, Agnew said that a two-percent-per-$100 rise in the state property tax suggested in his budget message—although he had campaigned against a tax increase—had originated in Goldstein's office. Goldstein retorted that he was against the hike.

Agnew asked Burch for an opinion on the constitutionality of a little-used state strike law "whether I'm going to invoke it or not." Burch said he was too busy to undertake lengthy research "only to satisfy idle curiosity."

Agnew was so new to the ways of Annapolis he was startled when reporters paid him the traditional courtesy of rising at his first press conference. Yet then—as now—he had his differences with the press. When, at the end of his first year as governor, reporters wrote that he had underestimated state income, Agnew struck back with an angry accusation that the press had not even covered the assembly's committee hearings on state revenue, a charge which later proved false.

His friend and campaign manager, George White, believes there was a misunderstanding all the way around. He says State Comptroller Louis Goldstein, a Democrat, had "deliberately misled" Agnew by forecasting a lower revenue figure, thereby forcing Agnew, a Republican new to state government, to make embarrassing and unnecessary economies. He says Agnew's anger was directed first at Golstein and secondly at the press for not making that point more forcefully. Since it had been disclosed at committee hearings, he said Agnew charged reporters "must not have" been present.

Herb Thompson has still another version.

He says Assembly Speaker Marvin Mandel, who was later to succeed Agnew as governor, tipped off Frank DeFlippio of the *News-American* and Jonathan Cottin of the *Evening Sunpaper* that Paul Cooper, head of financial research for the state, intended to "take on" Agnew when Cooper testified before the Assembly's Revenue Committee later in the day.

Both men wrote stories to that effect and were dismayed when Cooper failed to make good on Mandel's promise. It was too late then to recall their earlier stories.

Agnew was angry and accused them of not even being present. What the then-govenor did not understand—and would now—is that reporters facing a deadline sometimes feel they must write advance stories and gamble they will be right, Tomspon says.

Agnew had already made Herb Thompson, the Associated Press' Annapolis Bureau Chief, his press secretary and later brought him to Washington. The dailies remained suspicious. When Agnew began holding weekly press conferences for weekly newspapers, their suspicions were confirmed; they were convinced this was his way of getting even. Reporters for the big dailies could attend, but they were embargoed from printing their stories until they had appeared in the weeklies. Thompson says the idea originated with Stanley Blair, whose Harford county has no daily, and he "sold it to Agnew."

But these were squalls on an otherwise calm sea. Agnew got along surprisingly well with the Democratic legislature; he was accustomed, in Baltimore County, to dealing with a Democratic council. He knew, instinctively, how to move men whose eyes were on the next election.

Yet he managed to impress some as more of an administrator than a politician, the type of technician brought in occasionally by governments of all parties all over the world because of their competence. The *Sun* remarked in a political roundup that Maryland's new governor "abhorred" speechmaking. This must have a strange sound to the heads of the TV networks, to the editiors of *The New York Times* and *Washington Post,* to the "effete snobs," who have been seared in Agnew's speeches since he became Vice-President.

Back at the mansion, things seemed to be going well. After four days, Judy Agnew reported that the only member of the family that had not made the adjustment was Connie, the family Kerry Blue terrier. The new governor referred to her fondly as Maryland's First Dog. Connie felt more like a prisoner. In Towson she had had the run of their ten-room home. There were certain areas off-limits to her at Government House, the state's offical residence for its governor. These, apparently, were the areas Connie preferred. She pouted. She sometimes misbehaved. Eventually, the family built her a playpen under the dining-room windows. Agnew seems always to have had a dog in his life. One of his early photographs is of him romping with a dog he called Frisky.

Mrs. Agnew had grown accustomed to the large household staff, even to the cooks who had served past governors. Governor Agnew was especially fond of her spaghetti sauce but she graciously agreed to the chef's suggestion that the governor might also like his.

Agnew also felt, she said modestly, that "my imperial crab is the best he has ever eaten anywhere." She prepared it as often as she could, but public life cut down on her kitchen duty considerably. Susan, however, prided herself on being an excellent cook and looked forward to the evenings when her parents were away. Then she insisted on cooking for the "family," and the kitchen staff, not averse to a night off, was quick to agree. Susan's cooking ran to steak, potatoes, and salads.

There were squalls about the mansion, too. Mrs. Agnew had used the same hairdresser in Towson for fifteen years; now she had to find another she liked in Annapolis. But even more of a jolt was the fact that their goings and comings were public property.

In Towson they had entertained when they felt like it. Mostly, Mrs. Agnew remembers, "other people entertained us."

Now, a Washington society writer sniffed, Judy Agnew, the new governor's wife, was "very low key about clothes." She was "seemingly indifferent" to name designers.

The *Washington Star* confided that Judy Agnew, at forty-seven, "wages the same battle of the bathroom scales with the same good intentions that thousands like her wage year-in-and-year-out. Like them, she had known defeat as often as she has known victory."

The big blowup, however, was the Battle of the Peanut-Butter Jars and/or Glasses.

In the middle of the 1968 Presidential campaign, society writers for all three Washington dailies reported the Agnews had scandalized Maryland society by serving martinis in peanut-butter glasses.

"My dear," the *Washington Post* quoted one outraged dowager, "I *know* a peanut-butter jar when I see one."

She did not explain how she knew.

Pandemonium ensued.

Herb Thompson, formerly AP's inperturbable chief who had since become Agnew's unflappable press secretary, was furious. He complained in a letter to the *Washington Daily News* that its society writer, Clare Crawford, had "gone to great length to try to embarrass Mrs. Spiro T. Agnew. . . . She has spread through the women's national press corps a vicious, malicious, and totally false story that the Agnews serve drinks in Government House in peanut butter glasses.

The story had been that former Governor Tawes ate a peanut-butter sandwich every night before going to bed, and that the glasses had just accumulated.

Mrs. Agnew went on television at the height of the storm to prove that *her* glasses were not Tawes's leftovers. She brought along samples of her crystal to prove her point.

"It upset Mrs. Cain [Anne Cain, housekeeper at Governor's House]." She said by way of explaining why she was upset, "We had a cocktail party one night and ran out of just plain cocktail glasses. So we got ordinary glasses from the kitchen. I think they're called the Cape Cod pattern. If peanut butter comes in them, it must be pretty expensive. As a matter of fact," she concluded triumphantly, "the peanut butter we use comes in screw-top jars."

Now the search for truth was on in full cry. Girl reporters invaded the Government House pantry to discover who was and who wasn't telling it like it was. Lining the shelves of Mrs. Cain's upstairs pantry they found Cape Cod pattern pressed-glass footed goblets, juice glasses, sherberts, and salad plates. They could, one lady reporter noted, be found in most department stores for about "$2 apiece."

Obviously, they decided, the Agnews' glasses had been confused with glasses from Big Top Peanut Butter. Some of the ladies even traced down Baltimore representative of Procter and Gamble which made Big Top Peanut Butter. Reluctantly—he first inquired as to their politics—he produced some. Pictures were taken.

"The resemblance is so close," Clare Crawford wrote, "that anyone could mistake one for the other if they weren't side by side. In fact, it is hard to understand why anyone would be upset over the mistaken identity."

Mrs. Crawford, one of Washington's ablest reporters, is also the wife of Maryland State Senator Victor Crawford. Although they are Democrats, they were friendly with the Agnews. She was still miffed at Thompson's charge that she had spread "vicious, malicious, and totally false" stories about the Agnews. She put the blame squarely on Herb Thompson, where, by feminine logic, it so properly belonged.

Thompson, she said, was at the party and had been present when the glassware was being discussed but "he did not dispute the peanut-butter-origin theory at the time."

Mrs. Agnew had other crosses to bear, however.

On the eve of the Nixon Inauguration, the *Montgomery County Sentinel*, a Democratic paper, carried a story that she had squandered all of the $20,000 the state of Maryland annually appropriates to maintain Government House, leaving nothing for Mrs. Marvin Mandel, wife of the new governor.

Actually, Judy Agnew had carefully accounted for the money to the last penny and just as carefully deposited it in a special account in an Annapolis bank. But she had forgotten to tell anyone!

The matter was straightened out, and the *Sentinel* apologized. But Mrs. Agnew was badly shaken.

"Two things have upset her that I can remember," says Herb Thompson, whose wife Ann doubles as Mrs. Agnew's press secretary three days a week now that she is in Washington, "that story and the one about the peanut-butter glasses."

And, of course, there was the matter of the cultured pearls.

When South Vietnamese vice-president (and air marshal) Nguyen Cau Ky and his former air-stewardess wife came to Washington, it fell to Mrs. Agnew to entertain Mme. Ky. Randy had brought her a thirty-dollar strand of Hong Kong cultured pearls in a PX near Danang. As a "nice gesture" and to remind Mme. Ky of her homeland, Mrs. Agnew decided to wear them. Mme. Ky showed up literally dripping authentic pearls, some as big as hailstones.

Peanut butter out of the way, Agnew turned his attention to a strike of tugboat men in Baltimore harbor, which had lasted for twenty-three months. Agnew decided to mediate it. He offered his Baltimore conference room for negotiations and sat in with the two parties around the clock. The one-time attorney for the Amalgamated Meat Cutters and Butcher Workmen of North America, AFL-CIO, was no stranger to labor disputes. He knew where each side was vulnerable, and he knew how to get at that point.

He coupled his generosity with a threat to order a full state investigation of the dispute, a probe the union, at that particular point in time, wanted at all costs to avoid.

The strike was promptly settled.

Agnew, early in his administration, had doubled the size of his executive staff. Governor Tawes, a small-town banker, had operated before him with a small group of trusted friends. Agnew brought in what the *Baltimore Sun* described as "loyal, bright, and for the most part young men."

His first year had gone well. It had, in fact, gone swimmingly, and Agnew was politician enough to have misgivings about that. It was not a normal state of political affairs and it could not last.

He was lonely. There were the usual ribbon-cuttings, meetings with 4H Clubbers, presentations of awards, but his family was away. When summer came, the state began a $350,000 renovation of Government House. The governor moved aboard the state yacht, moored nearby, with a skeleton staff of servants. Mrs. Agnew and the family took a house at Ocean City. Judy was homemaker enough and Ted still enough of "her kind of man" that she came back to Annapolis weekly to look after him, convinced no servant, however loyal and well trained, could do the job she could.

"He's My Kind of Man, Ted Agnew Is" was Agnew's campaign song. Agnew found it a 'little silly" but was delighted when, for instance, workers in a packing plant greeted him with it. "They know me!" he exclaimed.)

The Agnew gift to the renovation was a sauna bath. Mrs. Agnew seldom used it because she said it did things to her hair. "Maybe I should use it Monday nights," she said. "I go to the hairdresser on Tuesday." She never did.

Agnew was approaching the turning point of his administration. Liberal support is an inconstant thing with a quicksand base. The euphoria of having elected one they considered their own had begun to wear off. Liberal uneasiness with Agnew already had a good start. His 1968 budget had faced realities and cutbacks were the order of the day. He cut, among other things, health, higher education, and welfare appropriations. And he cut them drastically. A Democratic state senator denounced him on the floor of the legislature as the "East Coast version of Ronald Reagan."

In Washington, previously all-Negro Howard University was in turmoil. Classes were suspended when rioting broke out just before semester examinations. Buildings were occupied. Tensions leaped thirty miles down the parkway into Baltimore whose Negro middle class supplied a sizable part of Howard's enrollment.

Bowie State College lies between Washington and Baltimore, close by the racetrack of the same name, within shouting distance of the multimillion-dollar housing development Levitt & Sons had built there and named Belair. Few Negroes live in Belair; civil-rights people occasionally picket it, but nothing seems to change.

Bowie State was once a teachers college. It is still preponderantly Negro though it has a heavy night-school enrollment of older whites. Bowie State was run down. Its dorms were leaky, its buildings in disrepair. It was hardly Spiro Agnew's fault. The neglect extended back through several administrations.

Inspired by the demonstrations at Howard, Bowie's student leadership went into action.

The trouble at Bowie State had begun innocently enough when its president, Dr. Samuel Myers, went to Morgan State College in Baltimore to deliver an address. (He was due to go on vacation the next day.)

At three A.M., Herb Thompson, Agnew's press secretary, got a call from Dr. Myers at his Annapolis home. Myers said the students had seized the campus, occupied the administration building and refused him admittance.

Thompson suggested he wait until six when he would call Governor Agnew and let Dr. Myers talk with him. At six A.M.

Myers told Agnew what had happened, and concluded with "I need your help."

"You'll have it," Governor Agnew assured him. "The state police will be there."

Agnew then called the Maryland State Police barracks at Waterloo, near Bowie, and told the officer in charge to take "however many men are necessary, go to that campus, take back the administration building, and turn it over to Dr. Myers." He cautioned, however, that he did not want unwarranted force used.

During most of the day, the state police remained off campus and tried to negotiate with the militants. At midafternoon Agnew received a call from State's Attorney Arthur Marshall of Prince Georges County, a Democrat, who told Agnew that he could not arrest the students because they were violating no state law. Agnew reminded him that they had turned on all the water taps and electric lights, had seized the switchboard and were making long-distance calls indiscriminately.

At dusk, the state police moved onto the campus and took possession of all buildings.

Three days later Bowie State students chartered four buses and went to Annapolis to protest conditions at the school. Agnew had warned them and their faculty they would be arrested if they disregarded state law. When the capitol was closed at five P.M. the students were advised they faced arrest. Bowie State faculty members pleaded with them to leave. When they refused, they were arrested. Charges against them were later dismissed, however.

Agnew said that the student protest at Bowie occurred despite the fact that he had doubled its appropriations in his first year in office.

To Governor Agnew it was a simple case of breaking the law. If one man had refused to leave the capitol building at 5 P.M. he would have been arrested. What difference if there were 227?

He ordered their arrest, all 227 of them.

Liberals were appalled. To them it was not that simple. The demonstrators were "orderly" (a questionable point of semantics to those who were trying to work in the capitol). They caused no disturbance. They were exercising a "constitutional right."

Ted Agnew did not see it that way. Disturbances were caused, he said, "not by evil conditions but by evil men."

He promptly closed down Bowie State. It was reopened sometime later and has been remarkably quiet and trouble-free. State money has since been allocated for its rehabilitation.

Some mark this as the turning point in the Agnew administration.

"I was for him—he was a good governor—until Bowie State," a liberal-oriented reporter on a Baltimore daily said recently.

But all this was prelude.

Dr. Martin Luther King, the greatest Negro leader of them all, was assassinated in Memphis in April, 1968.

Washington and Baltimore erupted. Much of the Negro district in the nation's capital was put to the torch. Scores were killed. The main business district was invaded by angry blacks, stores looted and burned. Frightened whites fled to the suburbs. President Lyndon Johnson watched tensely from his White House command center. Martial law was declared.

Baltimore reacted in the same way. Fires destroyed whole business and residential blocks. People were killed. Agnew, in Annapolis, called out the National Guard. The disturbances went on for days.

At the peak of the trouble Agnew called Negro leaders to his Baltimore office, presumably for a conference. He was coldly furious. Those he called for could be classified as moderates. Some were members of the assembly and authentic members of the establishment, though with a recognized political need to maintain their links with the militants.

He minced no words. That was not his way.

Hard on the heels of tragedy [he began in cold, measured tones], comes the assignment of blame and excuses. I did not invite you here for either purpose. I did not ask you here to recount previous deprivations, nor to hear me enumerate prior attempts to correct them.

The assembled black leaders stirred uneasily. This was not what they had expected. Agnew went on.

Look around you and you may notice that everyone here is a leader, and that each leader present has worked his way to the top. If you'll observe, the ready-mix, instant type of leader is not present.

The circuit-riding, Hanoi-visiting type of leader is missing from this assembly.

The caterwauling, riot-inciting, burn-American-down type of leader is conspicuous by his absence.

That is no accident, ladies and gentlemen. It is just good planning. All in the vernacular of today—"That's what it's all about, baby."

Some weeks ago, a reckless stranger to this city, carrying the credentials of a well-known civil-rights organization, characterized the Baltimore police as "enemies of the black man." Some of you here, to your eternal credit, quickly condemned this demagogic proclamation. You condemned it because you recognized immediately that it was an attempt to undermine lawful authority—the authority under which you were elected and under which you hold your leadership position. You spoke out against it because you knew it was false and was uttered to attract attention and inflame.

They had settled back now, pleased by the compliments, proud that the governor recognized them as responsible leaders. Agnew went on.

When you, who courageously slapped hard at irresponsibility, acted you did more for civil rights than you realize. But when white leaders openly complimented you for your objective, courageous action, you immediately encountered a storm of censure from parts of the Negro community. That criticism was born of a perverted concept of race loyalty and inflamed by the type of leader whom I mentioned earlier is not here today.

Frowns had begun to replace smiles. Agnew continued.

And you ran. You met in secret with that demagogue and others like him—and you agreed, according to published reports that have not been denied, that you would not openly criticize any black spokesman regardless of the content of his remarks.

You were beguiled by the rationalizations of unity; you were intimidated by veiled threats; you were stung by accusations that you were "Mr. Charlie's boy," by epithets like "Uncle

Tom." God knows I cannot fault you who spoke out for breaking and running in the face of what appeared to be overwhelming opinion in the Negro community. But actually, it was only the opinion of those who depend upon chaos and turmoil for leadership—those who deliberately were not invited here today. It was the opinion of a few distorted minds and magnified by the silence of most of you here today.

The Negro leaders were angry now. From the back of the room came a shout: "If you want to talk to us as ladies and gentlemen, Mr. Governor, we'll stay and listen."
Agnew went on:

Now, parts of many of our cities lie in ruins. You need not have to leave these city limits to verify the destruction and the resulting hardship to our citizens.
And you know who the fires burned out, just as you know who lit the fires.
They were not lit in honor of your great fallen leader. Nor were they lit from an overwhelming sense of frustration and despair. Those fires were kindled at the suggestion and with the instruction of the advocates of violence. It was no accident that one such advocate appeared at eight separate fires before the fire chief could get there.
The looting and the rioting which has engulfed our city during the past several days did not occur by chance. It was no mere coincidence that a national disciple of violence, Mr. Stokely Carmichael, was observed meeting with local black power advocates and known criminals in Baltimore on April 13, 1968—three days before the Baltimore riots began.
It is deplorable and a sign of sickness in our society that the lunatic fringes of our black and white communities speak with wide publicity while we, the moderates, remain continuously mute.
I cannot believe that the only alternative to white racism is black racism.

They were quieter now, but angry, waiting to hear what would come next.

Somewhere the objectives of the civil-rights movement have been obscured in a surge of emotional oversimplification. Somewhere the goal of equal opportunity has been replaced by the goal of instantaneous economic equality. The country does not guarantee that every man will be successful, but only that he have an equal opportunity to achieve success.

did allow his own way.

It was pure Agnew, self-made man, son of a Greek immigrant who had forged his own way.

> I readily admit that this equal opportunity has not always been present for the Negroes—that it is still not totally present for Negroes.
>
> But I say that we have come a long way. And I say that the road we have trodden is built with the sweat of the Roy Wilkens [of the National Association for the Advancement of Colored People] and Whitney Youngs (of the National Urban League) with the spiritual leadership of Dr. Martin Luther King—and not with violence.
>
> Tell me one constructive achievement that has flowed from the madness of the twin priests of violence, Stokely Carmichael and Rap Brown. They do not build—they demolish. They are agents of destruction, and they will surely destroy us if we do not repudiate them and their philosophies—along with the white racists such as Joseph Carroll and Connie Lynch [two Maryland white supremists]—the American Nazi party, the John Birchers and their fellow travelers.

Governor Agnew paused to quote from Carmichael (now in voluntary exile) and Brown (whereabouts unknown). He quoted Willard Dixon from a publication known as *"The Black Dispatch*—a voice from the Black Ghetto."

" 'Black people are being forced to become both judge and jury. We must arm ourselves with rifles, shotguns, pistols, bows and arrow (with poison arrows), BB guns (with poison BBs), gas, rags, bottles, and knives. The only way to get justice in this evil land is to kill the white devil before he kills you.' "

Negro leaders had begun to walk out. In all, fifty-nine of approximately 100 left before Agnew concluded. But he went on.

> What possible hope is there for peace in our country if these apostles of anarchy are allowed to spew hatred unchallenged?

If we are to learn from bitter experience, if we are to progress in the battle for equal opportunity, we must plan together and execute these plans together. To do this, we must be able to communicate. We cannot communicate and progress if the lunatic fringes are included on the problem-solving team.

I publicly repudiate, condemn, and reject all white racists. I call upon you to publicly repudiate, condemn, and reject all black racists.

This, so far, you have not been willing to do.

I call upon you as Americans to speak out now against the hate of Stokely Carmichael and Rap Brown. If our nation is not to move toward two separate societies—one white and one black—you have an obligation, too.

I submit to you that these men and others like them represent a malignancy out of control; that they will lead us to a devastating racial civil war. I submit to you that there can be no winner from such a conflict, and that the heaviest losers will be the Negro citizens of America.

It is not too late to return to the true target of the crusade for equality. That target is the elimination of all prejudice against Negroes in America and the provision of an equal opportunity to reach the top. That target will be realized when every man is judged on his own individual merit and only on his merit. Divisiveness and the doctrine of apartheid are barriers between us and that target. With your help they can be torn down.

About half the Negro leaders still sat in their seats. They listened quietly. Agnew continued:

I am sure that these remarks come as somewhat of a surprise to you; that you expected nebulous promises and possibly a light endorsement of the Kerner report. This I could not do. Some hard things needed to be said. The desperate need to confront the problem squarely justified the political risk in saying them.

I need your help, but your help would be of little value if you did not know and subscribe to the objectives for which I seek it. We can do much together, little apart. Blind militancy must be converted into constructive purpose. This cannot occur so long as you or I condone or cling to racism, black or white. We do not deserve the mantle of leadership, unless we are prepared to wear it proudly and, if need be, defiantly.

Above all, I believe you represent the views of the overwhelming majority of Maryland's Negro citizens—responsible, hardworking, decent people who are as horrified by the events of the past days as you or I. These are the people who will be unjustly victimized by a hardening of attitudes in the responsible, decent white community—white people who clearly repudiated racism in the 1966 election—white people who could normally be expected to indorse the 1967 open-housing legislation on referendum this November.

My greatest fear is that this polarization of attitudes is an aftermath of violence. Next I fear that we cannot endure continuous tension over the next months—that our community cannot live in constant fear that any irrational provocation may cause racial war.

Together we must work first to prevent polarization and second to reduce tension. I will need your vision and your voice. Now as never before your articulate, responsible leadership is needed. I am prepared to do whatever I can to aid the innocent victims of last week's rampage, to alleviate clear abuses and to enlarge opportunity within the inner city.

We must do this—as I said in my report to the people last Sunday night—"not out of a fear of reprisal but out of certain faith that it is right."

So let us begin to rebuild the image of Baltimore. Let us work together—not as black and white—but as responsible citizens of Maryland who uphold the law; as concened citizens who are united in their dedication to eliminate prejudice and poverty and any conditions which create hopelessness and despair.

He was nearing the end. He had said—was saying—what he felt had to be said. He felt what he said was reasonable and right, expressed with restraint. But he had no illusions what the initial reaction would be. He had seen them walk out. He knew their pride was bruised, their dignity offended. He could only hope that—over the long haul—his words would sink in and he would get the help for which he was pleading.

Let us publicly and promptly renounce any who counsel or condone violence. Let us acknowledge that we have a real stake in our society. Let us proudly acclaim our patriotism and our recognition that no nation in the world offers such opportunity. The fiction that Negroes lack any opportunity in this country is dispelled by the status of those of you in this room.

As Thomas Jefferson said nearly two centuries ago, "With all the imperfections of our present government, it is without comparison the best existing, or that ever did exist."

Agnew walked away, while the Negro leaders met in the hallway and drew up their own statement. Some were furious; others were near tears.

"We are shocked at the gall of the governor," their statement began, "suggesting that only he can define the nature of leadership in the black community. Agnew's actions are in keeping with the slave system of a bygone era. . . ."

"He talked to us like we were children," State Senator Verda Welcome (D.-Baltimore) said furiously. "So few whites understand black people."

Said the Reverend Marion C. Bascom. "He's as sick as any bigot in America. He's as sick as any bigot I've every known."

As he had known it would, reaction came swiftly. Liberal newspapers up and down the East Coast were critical. Baltimore Mayor Thomas D'Alessandro rushed into print with the statement that he had urged Governor Agnew to modify his "inflammatory statement." "We should be emphasizing reconciliation and harmony, not divisiveness," he said. Dr. Gilbert Ware, the top Negro in the Agnew administration, felt compelled to say he had not seen the statement in advance, and had not attended the meeting.

"Don't you think I knew I was committing political suicide?" Agnew retorted. For once, he was never more wrong.

They offered him an "out." The governor, they said, was exhausted after many sleepless nights. He spoke without thinking. Thompson let it be known that Agnew had written the message himself after much deliberation. Agnew read over the speech the next morning and found it "excellent" and "appropriate." So did others, apparently. Of 1,039 tele-

a whites on blacks

grams and 298 telephone calls to the governor's office, only 63 condemned him.

The *Baltimore News-American* said editorially. "One thing we like about Governor Agnew is his determination to put the blame where it belongs, with no pussyfooting circumlocution and no white-washing evasion. Many do not agree with him, but the governor is a man with the courage of his convictions."

After the speech, Negro students, presumably from Bowie State, left a sheet and a bullwhip, symbols of the Ku Klux Klan, spread over the fence at the governor's mansion.

Some liberals noted a "hardening" of Agnew's position on race relations after that. He seemed to miss no opportunity to denounce civil disobedience and "the wave of permissiveness sweeping this country"—and in language much of the nation wanted to hear. Asked at a press conference about minority demands for a "just share" of the nation's affluence and dignity, he replied.

"There cannot be such a thing as a just share of wealth. Some have more wealth than others. Sometimes it's circumstance that brings about such disparities, sometimes it's lack of effort. But, whatever the reason, we cannot have equal wealth.

". . . I have always felt that dignity is a quality developed internally by the individual. It is not something you buy and apportion like ice cream."

Hard on the heels of the April riots and his break with the Negro community—it took Maryland out of the Nixon-Agnew column in 1968—came another defeat. But this one he shared with every other political leader in the state.

Maryland's constitution, adopted in 1867 and amended 203 times since, was a hodgepodge. Under it the executive was fragmented, the judiciary scrambled, the legislature inefficient. Maryland's counties were under state control with an assembly spending most of its time on local bills, much as Congress runs the District of Columbia.

In 1965, Tawes had named a nonpartisan study commission. Chaired by a respected Baltimore attorney, H. Vernon Eney, it recommended a complete overhaul. The voters approved a referendum calling for a constitutional convention, and in September, 1967, one convened in Annapolis.

Maryland's constitutional convention was strictly nonpartisan. Few elected officials were among the delegates, most of whom were leading civic, legal, and professional leaders chosen for their knowledge rather than party affiliation. Delegates were seated alphabetically rather than by county.

The document that came out of the sessions was hailed across the country as one which would not only free Maryland from nineteenth-century rule but serve as a model for other states. It provided a unified court system, a streamlined executive, and mandatory county home rule. The voting age was dropped from twenty-one to nineteen. It was approved by a vote of 133 to 3, and signed by all but two of the delegates, one fatally ill and one who had broken his hand.

Agnew took the lead in the drive for ratification. In an unprecedented press conference he shared with heads of the state's judicial and legislative branches, they emphasized their united support of the new charter. The state's two living ex-governors, Tawes and McKeldin, joined in. So did Maryland's two Democratic senators, Daniel Brewster and Joseph D. Tydings. It had the support of two-thirds of the legislature, six out of seven congressmen, and civil, professional, and business leaders.

By comparison, the opposition was fragmented, led by unknowns. They were county clerks, sheriffs, and court clerks whose positions were less secure under the new charter. Organized labor grumbled a bit that the right to organize had not been sufficiently guaranteed. Some worried about costs; the opposition said its implementation would take $153 million the first year. Supporters said it would take but $3 million. After the April riots, some voters apparently were afraid to trust young people with the vote.

Agnew and Eney hoped for a heavy turnout—and they got it. Fifty percent of Maryland's 1.4 million voters turned out on May 14, 1968. When the votes were counted, the new constitution had lost, 366,575 votes to 283,050. Seldom had the whole leadership of any state been so resoundingly slapped down.

But 1968 was an election year, and Agnew's attention was focused more and more on who would be his party's nominee for the Presidency. The Democrats were in trouble. The Republicans had a golden opportunity to take over the White House. Although Agnew had been in politics less than ten years, and only five in elective office, he was determined to have a voice in who the new occupant would be.

V

SEARCH FOR A CANDIDATE

At San Francisco in 1964, Agnew was one of seven Maryland delegates who refused to switch to Barry Goldwater and cast their votes all the way for Pennsylvania Governor William Scranton.

His support of Goldwater in the race against Johnson was somewhat less than enthusiastic. "I would have preferred a more progressive candidate," he said.

Now, approaching the 1968 elections, he found himself being tarred with the same brush. As far as the liberals were concerned, his speech to the Negro leaders on April 11 had banished him into outer darkness. He was expected to support a Goldwater-type conservative.

Agnew still considered himself a progressive, if not a liberal.

So did his supporters.

Theodore Roosevelt McKeldin was, and is, Maryland's Mr. Republican. His liberal credentials are unchallenged. Twice governor of Maryland, twice mayor of Baltimore, he placed President Eisenhower's name in nomination at Chicago. He bolted the party only once—to support Johnson against Goldwater.

McKeldin has said: "They're wrong when they say Governor Agnew has shifted to the right. We still share pretty much the same attitudes. He was concerned about the April riots, and properly so. We all were. Some say he made a serious political mistake by calling the Negro leaders in and talking to them as he did . . .

"All that did was to make him Vice-President of the United States.

"He's opposed, of course, by a certain element in this country. But that element is very, very small. It is vocal, but a minority. He can afford to ignore them."

At San Francisco, Agnew had been Baltimore County executive. Now he was governor and certain to head the Maryland delegation to Miami Beach where the Republican

63

ticket would be chosen. No one could challenge him for that role, for Maryland, then without a Republican in the U.S. Senate, had only three Republican members in the House. As Ted Agnew went, so would the Grand Old Party of Maryland.

He began looking around for a candidate.

When battle lines were still forming, Agnew attended a Republican governors' conference at Jackson Hole, Wyoming. This was in May of 1967. Agnew had been governor for five months. Rockefeller tried to line up all GOP governors behind Romney. He made a special pitch to Agnew, and, for a while, Agnew felt he might do as Rockefeller—who was his candidate—asked. Romney's record as a businessman—he had been president of American Motors—and as a vote-getter in his home state impressed Agnew.

Romney had been first in the field. He waged a vigorous, well-financed campaign. But his mercurial temperament, his changes of mood and position were alien to Agnew, who held to a stand once he took it.

Patriotism was a sacred word to this son of a Greek immigrant. He used it in his speech on the April riots to Maryland's Negro leaders. His disillusionment with Romney became complete when the Michigan governor, claiming he had been brainwashed on an earlier trip to Vietnam, came out against the war.

Agnew said disgustedly that such talk "makes me a little ill."

Agnew then turned to Governor Nelson Rockefeller of New York. He admired the New Yorker; his courageous defiance of rabid Goldwater supporters in San Francisco in 1964 had aroused Agnew's ingrained respect for the underdog. Rockefeller's record in Albany had been a progressive one.

Agnew denied that his unsolicited support of Rockefeller was designed to stop Romney, whom Rockefeller was supporting. He said Romney was a "potentially good candidate," but that Rockefeller was the "outstanding man we have."

At the National Governors' Conference held in Washington in 1967, Rockefeller was widely reported to be ready to announce his candidacy. Agnew called on him and urged him to do so. Agnew, by this time, had established himself nationally as a leader of the Draft-Rockefeller movement. Reporters were tripping over themselves to learn what he knew. Agnew enjoyed the experience.

In Annapolis on April 2, the headlines were "Agnew Solid for Rockefeller." The governor called the New Yorker "the most outstanding governor and national figure the Republican party has had in a generation."

Shortly thereafter, Agnew made his first speech for Rockefeller in New Haven, Connecticut. He was pleased with its reception, and particularly liked the national publicity it brought him.

Agnew's trips to New York to confer with Rockefeller became more and more frequent. Sometimes he was spotted in the hallways and besieged by the press. Other times he slipped in unnoticed. Apparently, Rockefeller did not attempt to discourage him. Each time Agnew came away with new determination.

In the meantime, Agnew had been introduced to Nixon in New York by State Senator Louise Gore, a wealthy Maryland conservative whom Nixon was later to make a UN delegate. Owner of the swank Jockey Club in Washington's Fairfax Hotel, with homes in exclusive Potomac, Maryland, Paris, and Annapolis, Miss Gore brought the two together and was delighted when they took to one another immediately. Miss Gore is the niece of liberal Democratic Senator Albert Gore (D.-Tenn.) with whom Agnew was later to exchange political insults. "Uncle Albert" once lived in the Fairfax, close by the apartment of Miss Gore's wealthy parents.

(In January, 1968, while Agnew was still for Rockefeller, he and Mrs. Agnew flew to New York to attend a National Republican Women's Club dinner at the Waldorf-Astoria. Louise Gore gave a reception later and invited Nixon to come by. She also asked Governor and Mrs. Agnew to drop by to meet Nixon. Their paths occasionally had crossed, but they had never talked together. Nixon had put in a plug for Agnew when he was running for governor. Appearing on *Meet the Press*, he had described Agnew as one of the GOP's "truly impressive candidates." At Miss Gore's reception, they sat across a coffee table and talked national and international affairs for two hours. All other conversation in the apartment died out. After Agnew left, Nixon turned to Miss Gore and remarked: "That governor of yours is quite a man. He should get around the country more."

On January 10, 1968, Agnew announced he was forming a

committee to draft Rockefeller for the Republican nomination. He found a "groundswell of public opinion" for Rockefeller and was "particularly impressed by the many prominent business, professional, and industrial leaders who are not active in politics" who were for him. Thompson says Rockefeller money was used to set up a Draft Rockefeller headquarters at 140 Main Street in Annapolis. George Hinman, Rockefeller's unofficial campaign manager, supervised its establishment, he says. Al Abrams, now administrative assistant to Senator Mathias of Maryland, was in charge.

The crucial date became March 21, 1968.

Governor Rockefeller had booked time on national television for an important announcement. Few questioned that he would declare for the Presidency again. Hinman called Abrams from New York to tell him to be sure and watch because Rockefeller would make an important announcement.

Rockefeller's telecast, by freak of circumstances, coincided with Agnew's weekly press conference. Thompson told him reporters would be sure to ask his reaction. Agnew shifted the press conference from his office to a larger conference room where there was a TV set.

Other statehouse politicians came in, and Agnew waved them expansively to be seated.

But Rockefeller did not announce. He withdrew.

"Quite frankly," he said over the tube while Agnew sat transfixed, "I want it clear at this time that the majority of party leaders want the candidacy of Richard Nixon at this time. It would, therefore, be illogical and unreasonable that I would try to arouse their support."

There was more, but he had said all Agnew needed to hear. Rockefeller said he had an obligation to the voters of New York who had just reelected him to a four-year term. He said the Republican party could not be served by "personal combat."

"Far from enlightening the nation or strengthening the party, such combat would prove abrasive and divisive," he said. "It would not be a healing race toward national purpose."

Agnew's poker face betrayed so little emotion most reporters were convinced Rockefeller had called him that morning and told him of his plans. But as the Governor of Maryland walked back to his office, out of the hearing of the press, he turned to his private secretary, Alice Fringer, and said:

"I feel like I've been hit in the stomach with a sledge hammer."

To the press he said, "The Governor of New York has spoken. I believe him, and I respect his reasons.

A week later, Thompson says, Agnew was privately importuned by Kentucky GOP Senator Thruston Morton to join another Draft Rockefeller campaign. In hot rage, he dashed off a telegram saying. "I will have no part of a Stop Nixon Movement."

Rockefeller said he had signed an affidavit withdrawing his name from the Oregon primary and had instructed his staff to respect his decision. He said he had sent telegrams to backers in Oregon informing them of his decision. He said, however, that his own positions on national and international affairs would be made known. "I must in good conscience do this."

Rockefeller seemed jaunty as he walked through midtown from his office to the Hilton for the broadcast, shaking hands along the way. He was wearing television makeup.

Ted Agnew was stunned. Rockefeller may have sent telegrams to unidentified backers in Oregon telling them of his decision, but he had neglected to place a call to the proud, stubborn man who had crawled so far out on a limb for him and was now left looking like a fool. Rockefeller to this day has not explained this lapse. It was an insult Agnew was never to forgive him.

Congressman J. Glenn Beall, Jr., then a member of the state assembly, was there. "I was never so sorry for a man," he recalls now. "He didn't lose his cool, but he was burned up, as I would have been, too."

The others left the room quietly, leaving Agnew to his bitter thoughts. Agnew was to deny later that what Rockefeller did on March 21 made any difference. Those who know him best believe differently. They know that beneath his sometimes bland countenance lurks a mercurial temper, usually under tight control. They know, too, that he is a man who places a premium on loyalty. At times thereafter he seemed almost to have lost faith in the words and promises of the liberals and moderates in his party. First Romney then Rockefeller had behaved in a manner incomprehensible to a

man who fought for the things he believed in without waver-
ing.

Rockefeller was not through, however. On April 30, 1968,
he changed his mind again and got back into the race. His
obligation to the people of New York who had just reelected
him governor somehow discharged in the previous forty days,
he said the Republican party deserved a choice. A month
before, he had said a fight for the nomination would be
"abrasive and divisive" and "serve no national purpose." He
now said comments from the sidelines were not enough.

Agnew was in Hawaii to dedicate a Sheraton Hotel and
did not bother to listen to Rockefeller's second TV speech.
Besides, he had troubles of his own. Back in Annapolis,
Thompson had told the press the governor was paying his
own expenses. He meant, he said later, no state money was
being used. A Sheraton press release said it was paying the
governor's expenses. Thompson had abjectly to confess error.
The *Baltimore Sun* unmercifully roasted both men in its
editorial columns.

"Today I announce my active candidacy for the nomination by the Republican party for President of the United
States," Rockefeller said with five former Republican national chairmen ostentatiously at his side. He then leaned over
and kissed his wife Happy.

"I do this because, first, dramatic and unprecedented
events have revealed the gravity of the crisis we face. A
comment from the sidelines in not the way to deal with this.
Men and women in all walks of life within the Republican
party and outsiders have urged me to take this step.

"Personally, I am deeply disturbed by the course of events,
the growing unrest and anxiety at home and abroad. By
taking this course at this time I feel I can best serve my
country. I shall do everything I can with all my energy now
and in the weeks before the convention."

Unmentioned was the fact that a month earlier President
Lyndon B. Johnson had announced he would not seek another term. Or Rockefeller may have been hoping for a draft
when he "withdrew" in March. When one did not material-
ize, perhaps he decided to take the plunge anyhow.

At any rate, this time he went without the governor of
Maryland at his side.

Eight days later, on March 29, Agnew flew to New York
for a luncheon with Nixon that lasted one hour and forty-five

minutes. Both men blandly insisted the question of his supporting the former Vice-President never came up. But the way Nixon's staff was parceling his time would seem to belie that. They would hardly allocate two hours to a discussion of the weather.

After the meeting, Agnew told the press: "I am not ready to announce any support for Mr. Nixon, but I have a high regard for him."

That was close enough for the time being.

By May 17, Agnew was being touted as a running mate for Nixon. This, of course, happened at one time or another during the campaign to every Republican officeholder of any consequence. It was flattering, but hardly taken seriously even in Maryland. Even after the Free State's delegation was safely bedded down in Miami Beach at the start of the convention, Frank DeFilippo, of the *Baltimore News-American,* reported that the remark most often heard was: "What a shame he's from Maryland."

A small eastern seaboard state, widely known as Washington, D.C.'s bedroom, presumably Maryland was not important enough to rate a place on the national ticket.

The governor's office in Annapolis said he was not interested in a national appointment.

Agnew, meanwhile, had become convinced that Nixon was the party's best hope. Without a formal declaration, he threw himself into the campaign for Nixon's nomination with all of the adrenaline and fervor that had characterized his past races. Rockefeller was spending millions from his personal fortune on television shorts that would indicate that the vast majority of the American people were ready to vote for him. Nixon was lining up support and votes. Agnew was in the middle of the effort.

It was becoming evident, however, that Rockefeller still had strength in Maryland. The Washington suburbs, traditionally mugwump, if not liberal, were determined to vote for him, as Agnew four years earlier had been determined to vote for Scranton. He was, in the final analysis, able to throw only sixteen of his state's twenty-six delegate votes to his choice, Nixon.

Nixon privately asked Agnew to place his name in nomination at Miami Beach. Agnew was delighted. As head of the Maryland delegation he was assigned a suite on one of the top floors of the Swank Eden Roc Hotel.

In Annapolis, when he had time, he mulled over his nominating speech. There were hurried telephone conferences with members of the Maryland delegation, each of whom had a problem that could only be solved by Ted. Since the majority were his friends and loyal backers, he took time to listen to them.

A week before he took off for Miami Beach he golfed at the Turf Valley Country Club in Howard County with his old friend Judge Barrett of Towson. Barrett remembers that Governor Agnew shot an 83—as low a game as he can remember him every shooting—while Barrett's score was a few strokes higher. Agnew's golf game had improved along with his political standing; he no longer need apologize for either.

Miami Beach is one of America's gaudiest pleasure spots. It is devoted almost wholly to pursuit of the almighty dollar and makes no bones about it. Billboards on the outskirts suggest that tourists bring dollars with them, and this is only partially in jest. There was a question in the minds of some Republicans whether the party—already accused of representing the fat cats—ought to meet in such an atmosphere.

It was carnival time. Each candidate tried to outdraw the other. Governor Rockefeller arrived on August 5 to a raucous and elaborate reception. There were other receptions and balls. Traffic was snarled. Hotel rooms had been booked long in advance. People who thought they rated—and did back home—were happy to settle for motel accommodations miles from the center of things. The wealthy who owned Florida homes opened them and threw bashes that were bedlam. Yachts and houseboats were made available to the few who had a chance someday to wind up as President of the United States.

Ted Agnew went to Miami Beach as one of three "favorite sons" on whom the outcome could depend. His support of Nixon was public knowledge. But there is a ritual to be followed in a convention, and until he declared himself Agnew was officially a questionmark. More authentic favorite sons were Governors James A. Rhodes of Ohio and Romney of Michigan. Both were standing firm. Romney, after withdrawing, had allowed his name to be entered by the Michigan delegation. What he would do was anyone's guess. Rhodes, a wise politician, was widely believed to be holding out for the best deal for Ohio—perhaps to be Nixon's Vice-

Presidential nominee—and with his uncanny sense of timing was sure to make the switch at the most propitious moment. Inexplicably, he didn't until it was too late.

Into all this came the Maryland delegation and the Agnews of Towson. Only Kim, now twelve, and Randy, in Vietnam, were not in the family party. Kim was bored by the whole affair. She stayed in Ocean City with friends.

Rockefeller was everywhere with his breezy "Hi'ya, fella." He and his entourage exuded a confidence that most newsmen discounted. Hughes Rudd of CBS, remarking on the frenzied buildup despite Nixon's almost prohibitive lead, referred to it as "the lull before the lull."

Nixon people were everywhere, in the lobbies and private penthouses, the conference rooms and the social gatherings. They were, like their leader, unobtrusive, careful, cautious— and coolly confident. Nixon automobiles met incoming delegates at the airport, drove them to their hotels, looked after their needs. No detail was overlooked.

Meanwhile, each arriving plane brought more delegates, press people, TV and radio crewmen, and many just plain hangers-on.

Nixon was staying on Long Island at Montauk, New York. He had begun writing his acceptance speech on the Pacific Coast two weeks earlier and was finishing it away from the noise and confusion of the convention. With him, scattered in nearby bungalows at the resort site, were H. R. Halderman, his chief of staff; Rose Mary Woods, his personal secretary; Partrick Buchanan, who had drafted the candidate's tough statement on law and order; and Ray Price, another speechwriter who had handled his speeches on Vietnam.

To the surprise of few—Rockefeller had been claiming he would remain on the ballot as a favorite son through the first ballot—Agnew came out for Nixon on August 5. He brought sixteen of Maryland's twenty-six delegates with him. The psychological effect was evident; Agnew had been the first chairman of the Rockefeller draft, now he was on record for Nixon. Rockefeller people tried to put the best possible face on the situation. Pennsylvania Governor Raymond Shafer said it "won't have any devastating effect." Colorado Governor John Love said it "wasn't all that bad." William E. Miller, the 1964 Vice-Presidential nominee and now a Rockefeller aide, said the loss of Agnew was "not fatal to us."

But there was no denying that it hurt.

Agnew said he favored Nixon because of his experience as Vice-President and legislator, and in world affairs.

"More important," he added, "is his ability to make hard decisions quickly and accurately."

It seemed to some like a direct slap at Governor Rockefeller.

New Mexico Governor David Cargo, who had been leaning toward Rockefeller, followed Agnew's lead later in the day.

Ronald Reagan announced the same day that he had taken the words "favorite son" out of his candidacy and would seek the Republican Presidential nomination in earnest. The former movie star said pressure from the eighty-six-man California delegation pushed him into the race. Nixon sources said it was an act of desperation.

There were some defections. Reagan was an old Goldwater man and had strong appeal. Representative James Gardner of North Carolina, his party's candidate for governor, was the first to go. Two Georgia delegates switched to Reagan. A Virginian switched from uncommitted to the Californian. Governor Paul Lexalt of Nevada agreed to second his nomination.

Rhodes and Romney continued to stand fast.

Nixon flew in from New York on August 6, the day before the convention opened, with the raw notes of his acceptance speech in his briefcase. His plane reached Miami International Airport around six P.M. After their plane had taxied to a stop, the former Vice-President and his wife emerged and threw their arms around their two daughters and Julie's then-fiancé, David Eisenhower, who had arrived the day before. In a brief speech to 700 people at the airport, Nixon said, "This is the end of one journey and the start of another that is going to lead us—we think— to new leadership for this nation."

His motorcade took him to the Hilton Plaza, his convention command post. and an even more elaborate welcome. When he arrived, 2,000 balloons were released by his advance men. Two bands on either side of the hotel entrance broke into a song called "Nixon's the One," a bouncy tune compounded in equal parts of "Take me Along" and "Bringing in the Sheaves."

On hand also was a large, confused elephant. The crowd was big and boistrous. The elephant stepped on a reporter's foot. Nixon girls in red-and-white shirts and blue mini-skirts shrieked.

Surrounded by Secret Service men, Nixon happily pushed through the crowd to an elevator and his suite. His command post on another floor had been set up in a sauna bath.

Nixon had entrusted his so-called Southern strategy to men like Senator Strom Thurmond of South Carolina, Howard "Bo" Calloway of Georgia, Senator John Tower of Texas, and Harry Dent, South Carolina Republican chairman, who is now a White House aide. All liked and, under other circumstances, might have supported Reagan. Now they headed out to block him. It was not difficult. By and large, Nixon's Southern support was holding firm. But there were rumblings, particularly about reports he might pick New York Mayor John Lindsay as his running mate. That kind of talk, said Mississippi Chairman Charles Reed, "scares the hell out of us."

The convention got under way. Ex-Senator Barry Goldwater, the 1964 standard-bearer, made a strong plea for party unity.

"We are not here to accuse and we are not here to divide," he said. "The target is not to be found in this convention hall in Miami; it is not to be found in the Republican party anywhere."

General Dwight D. Eisenhower addressed the convention by closed-circuit television from his hospital suite in Walter Reed Army Medical Center in Washington. Although the party platform was to call for a negotiated peace in Vietnam, Eisenhower took a more belligerent stand. The Communists, he said, "reach ruthlessly for domination over Southeast Asia." He deplored a "growing dispositon on the part of some of us to ignore these aggressive moves . . . to seek for surface accommodations. . . ."

Governor Daniel J. Evans of Washington State delivered the keynote address and charged that the Democrats had wasted 20,000 lives, despite which "we have not won in Saigon, cannot negotiate in Paris, and will not explain to the American people."

Nixon aides formally asked Agnew to nominate him. The speech was ready. His big moment came on August 7 when, with Senator Edward Brooke (R.-Mass.), the only Negro in the United States Senate, presiding, he stood under the kleig lights and spoke before millions of his fellow countrymen.

If there is anything predictable in this unpredictable time, it is that from this convention will emerge not just the standard-bearer of a grand old party, but the President of a brave new country.

We are a nation in crisis, victimized by crime and conflict, frustrated by fear and failure.

A nation torn by war wants a restoration of peace.

A nation plagued by disorder wants a renewal of order.

A nation haunted by crime wants respect for the law.

A nation wrenched by division wants a rebirth of unity.

If there is one cry that rings clear, it is the cry for a leader.

At this moment of history the Republican party has the duty to put forward a *man*—a man to not only match this moment but to master it.

We have that man!

He has spent years building his party. He has spent a lifetime serving his country.

He has fought throughout his political career for principle and he has not hesitated to pay the price of unpopularity in standing up for principle.

He has traveled the continents taking America's message to the world. He has shared in the decisions which shaped for America the Eisenhower era of prosperity, untainted by war, dissension, fear, lawlessness, or the threat of fiscal and moral chaos.

He knows what is needed to be President and what a President needs to be.

But it is not only his record of yesterday, it is his voice for tomorrow that matches this man to this moment.'

He says: "This is the moment of opportunity for America. We sense that opportunity when we put aside what's wrong with America and start looking at what's right with America." I believe that, don't you?

He says: "Let's stop apologizing for America's wealth and power. Instead let's use it aggressively to attack those problems that threaten to explode the world." Isn't that what this party stands for?

He says: "Let's stop apologizing for the success of free enterprise and instead work at spreading and sharing that success."

He says: "Right now change rules America. It's time for America to rule change." Don't *you* believe that?

He says: "To a crisis of the spirit, America needs an answer of the spirit."

What is the spirit of this man who seeks now to answer the nation's call?

Ask the people of New Hampshire, Wisconsin, Indiana, Nebraska, South Dakota, Oregon—and they will tell you of a man who took his case to the people, and put his prestige on the line in every primary.

Ask the people with whom he shared power in Washington, and they will tell you of a man who has the wisdom to comprehend history, and the foresight to anticipate it; the confidence to make hard decisions; the courage to keep cool before one man in Moscow or a mob in Caracas.

Ask the people who have known him throughout his lifetime, and they will tell you of a man of warmth and wit, his perspective enriched by the private years.

Ask the people of this convention, and they will tell you of a man who helped lead this party to its greatest victories in the past two decades, and who stood by the party and its candidate in their darkest hour.

And when the American people are asked in November, they will speak too:

For a man firm in upholding the law, and determined in the pursuit of justice.

For a man who can negotiate peace without sacrificing life, land, or liberty.

For a man who had the courage to rise up from the depths of defeat six years ago—and to make the greatest political comeback in American history.

For the one man whose life gives proof that the American dream is not a shattered myth and that the American spirit—its strength and sense and stability—remains firm.

The final test of a man who seeks the Presidency is not what he promises but what he can do; not what he says, but what he is.

The man I nominate tonight is a President.

When a nation is in crisis, and when history speaks firmly to that nation that it needs a man to match the times—you don't create such a man; you don't discover such a man; you *recognize* such a man.

It is my privilege to place in nomination for the office of President of the United States, the *one* man whom history has so clearly thrust forward—the one whom all America will recognize as a man whose time has come—the man for 1968—the Honorable Richard M. Nixon.

Meanwhile, rioting had broken out in Miami, across the causeway. It raged for two days and two nights. At least three people were killed, homes and businesses burned. It was all too reminiscent of the April riots in Baltimore, yet it seemed far away. Television cameramen delighted in showing riot scenes in juxtapositon with corpulent, overdressed, somewhat comical delegates with their silly hats and horns.

The lull before the lull was proceeding. There was a script to be followed, of course. In the best American tradion, a political convention is part ritual, part theater, part politics. Rockefeller and Reagan held out hope Nixon could be stopped on the first ballot, though they probably knew better. If he could be stopped there, they said, he would steadily lose strength thereafter. But even in the Rockefeller ranks there was dissension. Rocky believed Reagan's candidacy would help him. Senator Jacob Javits said it was "inconceivable" that they would depend upon a man like Reagan for anything.

After the oratory, after the parades, after the hoopla, the balloting began. Nixon was ahead from the start. It was over at 1:50 the next morning when Wisconsin cast its thirty votes for him, pushing him over the required 667 mark.

He wound up with 692 votes. Rockefeller had 277; Reagan, 182.

Reagan moved to make it unanimous. Rockefeller called with congratulations. Ted Agnew was happy. He had picked a winner. Now he would go back to Annapolis. But first he wanted a brief vacation, just himself and Judy.

He was not to get it.

He was on his way still.

VI

SURPRISE CHOICE

At 12:15 P.M., Thursday, August 9, 1968, the room phone in Spiro Agnew's Eden Roc suite began to ring. His private lines had already been removed.

Agnew picked it up and listened. The expression on his face became grave. To Mrs. Agnew his lips silently formed the words: "I'm it."

Into the phone, he said simply: "I'm greatly honored."

Spiro T. Agnew, governor of the Free State of Maryland, was to be his party's nominee for Vice-President of the United States. He had come a long way.

There were several others in the apartment, among them Thompson, Stanley Blair and Art Sohmers. It was Blair who first picked up the room phone. Rogers Morton was on the other end of the line. He asked to speak to Ted.

"Ted," Morton asked, "are you sitting down? Here's a friend who wants to talk with you."

The friend was Nixon; his message was that Agnew was to be his running mate. The party in Agnew's apartment had been watching television, and the last word they had was that their governor had been eliminated. His "I'm greatly honored" did not at first sink in.

"We thought," Thompson recalls, "the President was honoring protocol, that this was a courtesy call to tell him someone else had been chosen."

He knew the convention was to end that evening with the nomination of someone for the number-two spot, but Agnew had never considered himself a serious contender. True, he had been mentioned, but that was pro forma. Many people were mentioned; a politician of stature would have reason to feel hurt if he weren't. But there were too many things against him: Maryland's size and location, his comparative obscurity, the opposition of the liberals. "Don't you think I know I'm committing political suicide?" he had asked after dressing down Maryland's Negro leaders during the April riots.

He and Judy had planned to spend a few days at a resort hotel in Freeport Beach, The Bahamas, before going back to Annapolis. He already had reservations. He had nothing more on his mind than picking up the reins of the governorship and campaigning for his party's ticket—if asked.

How his selection came about seems pretty well agreed on by political correspondents who were in Miami Beach. *Newsweek* and *U.S. News and World Report*, at opposite ends of the political spectrum, have published substantially the same account.

When Richard M. Nixon was nominated for the Presidency in the early hours of August 9, he still had not decided whom he wanted to run with him. The selection would have to be someone who could add strength to the ticket.

Some of the delegates went out on the town after adjournment. Some went back to their hotels and to bed. Practically all slept late the next morning. After the last several days, they were exhausted.

Richard Nixon was not one of them. Back in his penthouse suite in the Hilton Plaza he called in his top staff people and a few others to begin a preliminary search for a running mate.

He said he had no personal choice and asked for suggestions.

One by one, names were dropped, most of them names that had been mentioned in earlier stories. Mayor Lindsay was one of the first to be brought into the discussion. Senator Mark Hatfield of Oregon was another; a leading dove, keynoter of past conventions, he would be attractive. There had been strong sentiment for a Nixon-Reagan ticket even while Reagan was seeking the Presidential nomination. Reagan's name was introduced. Romney was mentioned, as was Senator Charles Percy of Illinois. Massachusetts Governor John Volpe had openly campaigned for the job. Agnew's name came up. So did Governor Rhodes', Senator Howard Baker's (Tennessee), Senator Robert Griffin's (Michigan), and Representative George Bush's (Texas).

Nixon eliminated one name at the start—Bush. He was a first-term congressman and lacked experience. Nixon talked at great length about what he wanted in his Vice-President. He must be capable of succeeding to the job of President. He must be a unifying force. He spoke somewhat acidly of the "glamour boys," which, although he did not say so, eliminated Lindsay, Reagan, and, possibly, Percy.

The meeting broke up. Immediately a new group was ushered in. Mr. Nixon had been waiting for them. These were the movers and shakers of the party, the authentic Republican Establishment.

There was Barry Goldwater; his successor in the Senate, Paul Fannin; Jim Rhodes of Ohio; Richard Ogilvie, Republican candidate for governor of Illinois; Congressman Sam Divine of Ohio; Tom Dewey, his party's Presidential nominee in three past elections; House Whip Leslie Arends of Illinois; Congressman Donald Rumsfeld, who now heads the Office of Economic Opportunity; former Attorney General Herbert Brownell; Senator Thurmond; Governor Louie Nunn of Kentucky; Hawaii's Senator Hiram Fong; Senator Karl Mundt of South Dakota; and Lieutenant Governor Bob Finch of California. Finally, there was evangelist Billy Graham.

Again, Nixon outlined what he hoped to get in a running mate. National acceptability came first. Nixon would like a governor, if the right man could be found in their ranks. He wanted someone who understood urban problems.

Republican leaders were more concerned about pushing their own candidates, or with eliminating those they didn't like. Ogilvie made a strong pitch for Percy. Graham interjected that whoever the nominee was he should be a man of high moral character. Goldwater and Thurmond came out strongly against Lindsay.

It was 6:30 before Nixon went to bed. At nine A.M. he was up again, to meet with still another group. The late Senator Everett Dirksen killed whatever chance his Illinois colleague Percy might have. House leaders Jerry Ford of Michigan and Bob Wilson of California were still plugging Mayor Lindsay. Texas Senator John Tower was for Reagan.

At 9:30, the Secret Service got a preliminary alert to be prepared to cover four men—Lindsay, Reagan, Percy, and Hatfield. An hour later, Hatfield's name was taken off the list and Governor Volpe's put on. A few minutes before noon, Agnew's name was added.

Nixon had said he would announce his choice at noon. This meeting broke up at 11:05. Nixon went back into conference with Finch, his closest friend. The list had been narrowed to Volpe, Hatfield, Agnew, and Finch. Finch took himself out. Hatfield was soon to follow. Now it was Volpe and Agnew.

Shortly before noon, Nixon chose Agnew.

It was, he said later, "very, very close."

Nixon told Agnew he was sending a Secret Service detail to pick him up. Thereafter, it would be his shadow, day and night, for at least four years. He told Agnew to wait until it arrived, then to come to his suite. While waiting for his bodyguards, Agnew saw Nixon announce his selection on television, and smiled wryly at the gasps from the press.

Immediately the cry went up. "Spiro *who*?" Throughout the day, according to the *The New York Times* the next morning, delegates seethed and grumbled. This was particularly true of the party's moderate wing and those from the big urban centers. Agnew, the liberal Republicans said, was anti-Negro. He had been picked by Thurmond. He was part of the Southern strategy. He was a down payment on the political debt Nixon owed the South's growing Republican party.

Back in Nixon's suite, the two men shook hands and sat down to arrange for the formalization of Nixon's choice. Nixon asked who Agnew wanted to nominate him. The answer came without hesitation: Congressman Morton. It was a good one; not only was Morton Agnew's close friend, he had been Nixon's floor manager. Then came the job of picking seconders. Thompson says Mayor John Lindsay of New York was Agnew's first choice. He also asked for Senator Percy. Nixon added Senator John Power of Texas. Both men agreed to let ex-Senator Bill Knowland of California make a second speech, too.

At first, Lindsay's seconding speech was to have been third or fourth. Agnew thought it would be better if he made the first. Lindsay later agreed.

Nixon had arranged a press conference for Agnew. It was just as well, Thompson says now, because Agnew was still pretty much overwhelmed by events of the last two hours. Agnew met with the press, then went on television. His sense of humor did not desert him.

"I'll agree with you," he drawled, "that the name of Spiro Agnew is not a household word."

But he said he hoped to make it one in the next couple of months.

A major revolt was brewing. Traditionally, the Presidential

nominee has the right to pick his Vice-President. But this was 1968, and anything could happen. Angry liberals made Mayor Lindsay their first choice, but he would have none of it. The Lindsay boom seemed to center in the Pennsylvania delegation. Lindsay called the Pennsylvania state chairman, James Jordan, and asked that nothing be done to start a floor fight for him.

The grumbling continued, some of it for publication.

"Agnew was a compromise," Ogilvie told reporters.

"It is inconceivable that the Nixon people did not even check with us," said Congressman Jim Fulton, a Pittsburgh Republican who had voted with Agnew to the bitter end for Bill Scranton in 1964.

"This is not our strongest ticket," grumbled Senator Javits.

The moderates and liberals who had once adored Ted Agnew and had helped elect him governor were now actively seeking for a candidate to oppose him. They knew he could not be stopped. But they could embarrass Nixon for his selection.

George Romney stepped into the breach. He agreed to let his name be presented to the convention. He would not withdraw.

The convention was called to order at 7:30 P.M. The world now knew that Agnew was Nixon's choice; it also knew he would be opposed.

After the preliminaries were out of the way, Agnew's name was placed in nomination by Congressman Rogers C. B. Morton of Maryland, brother of the Republican senator from Kentucky and soon, like his brother before him, to become the Republican national chairman.

Morton's speech was brief and complimentary, reflecting Maryland's pride in having a spot on the national ticket. But it was overshadowed—as were all other speeches that night— by Mayor Lindsay's. Lindsay had agreed to second Agnew's nomination.

It was remarkable how little mention he made of Agnew. The thrust of his message was the Republican platform and its commitment to the big cities. It seemed at times even to argue with Agnew as Lindsay pointedly said that "without justice the rule of law has no meaning." It seemed almost to challenge Agnew to carry out the pledges of the party platform.

Its significance lay not in what Mayor Lindsay said but

that he said it at all. If the convention could be turned around—a highly unlikely proposition—he was the man to turn it. When Lindsay took the platform to second Agnew's nomination, the fight was over.

> I rise to second the nomination of Governor Spiro T. Agnew as the next Vice-President of the United States [he said].
>
> He has been an outstanding governor of the State of Maryland and his administration has fulfilled many of the purposes of the platform this convention has adopted.
>
> We wrote an intelligent, forward-looking platform on which our candidates will conduct forthright campaigns. Our platform pledges the Republican party to a vigorous effort to transform our cities into centers of opportunity and progress.
>
> Governor Agnew's chief responsibility as the nominee is to carry to the nation the Republican party's conviction that we must have a change of government if we are to change the conditions in our cities:
>
> That we in the metropolitan areas must have national support instead of bureaucratic interference.
>
> That we need a new system of relationships between federal and local governments; a concert of action to contend with the expansion of the suburban communities and the decline of the central cities.
>
> That we must understand that justice is the cornerstone of our republic, and that without justice, the rule of law has no meaning.
>
> And most important, the United States must have the kind of leadership under which the rights of minorities are sheltered by the power of the majority. For this is the only way a democracy can succeed.
>
> Our platform also presents a mandate for peace abroad; a prerequisite for progress at home.
>
> These are the commitments the Republican party has undertaken:
>
> Commitments to change the course of the country;
>
> To give it a leadership that can command our strength, a national purpose that compels us to do what is right for America;
>
> A commitment, finally, for change.
>
> Only with a change at the highest levels of our government can this country find itself again. Only then will we be able to

talk to each other again. Only then will the ideals of America be given eloquent expression.

Governor Agnew knows the implications of the challenges before us. He has been the chief executive of Baltimore County, which contains one of the nation's largest cities. As governor of Maryland, he has dealt with the problems of the suburbs that make up the fastest-growing metropolitan area in the United States.

And by his proximity to Washington, he has direct experience with the failures of this administration to the critical task of shaping the future of an urban America. Where they have failed, we must succeed. And, if we carry out the promise of our platform, we will succeed.

This, then, is the year when once more we can speak as one people. This is the year that a Republican administration can bring the freshness of change to a weary nation.

So let's address the American people as one party—eager to articulate the hopes and dreams of a free nation.

For last year's words belong to last year's language. But next year's words must be given another voice.

Mrs. Lindsay was to say more than a year later that she "wasn't very happy" when her husband seconded Agnew's nomination. Appearing on NBC's *Today* show, she told Barbara Walters on December 30, 1969: "It was one way for him to stay out of, you know, there was a lot of pressure being put on him to run for, to be a candidate for Vice-President. And he really and truly did not want to. And he . . . it was a way of just saying to these people that were trying to get this ball rolling that I think the President has the right . . . the nominee for President has the right to pick his own man and he is Mr. Agnew, and, okay then, as a liberal mayor of an Eastern city, I will go along with that, in order to try to unify this whole thing and try to bring them together.

"In hindsight, I don't know that I think it was perhaps the most happy occasion, but then again people do odd things. There is an old saying, 'Politics makes strange bedfellows.' I don't know . . . they sure make a lot of strange ones, in my book, sometimes."

She said she still did not approve of Vice-President Agnew, that her opinion of him had not changed.

After Agnew's name was placed in nomination, George

Abbott, Nevada state chairman, nominated Romney, and the roll call began.

When it was over, Agnew had 1,128 votes, Romney 186, and there were 28 pointed abstentions. Ted Agnew was his party's Vice-Presidential nominee, but the party was deeply divided. Romney, predictably, received a majority of Michigan's votes, but he also ran ahead of Agnew in Minnesota, Oregon, and Delaware. Pennsylvania gave Agnew 30 votes. Romney 24, and Lindsay 10. New York, held sternly in check by Rockefeller, gave Agnew 84 votes. But eight New York delegates defied their governor to vote for Romney.

Nixon tried to put the best possible face on the revolt. He said it was a "healthy thing."

Agnew, in his acceptance speech, was blunter. He spoke of the "improbabilities of the moment." He "fully recognized that I am an unknown quantity to most of you." But he did not trim his sails. Where Lindsay, in seconding his nomination, declared the rule of law has no meaning without justice, Agnew asserted that "anarchy and rioting [serve] no constructive purpose in a constitutional republic." At the same time he pledged to "make black Americans partners in our system."

What can I bring to this moment in behalf of our party and its great Presidential nominee? Well, perhaps a few objectives born of deep conviction:

The objective to analyze and help solve the problems of this nation without dependence on the canned philosophies of liberalism or conservatism.

The objective to avoid the currently popular concept that the only purpose of government is to spend money and that all spending in a good cause is worthy, whether or not it will get results.

The objective that racial discrimination, unfair and unequal education, and unequal job opportunities must be eliminated, no matter whom that displeases. And I believe quite compatibly the observation that anarchy, rioting, or even civil disobedience has no constructive purpose in a constitutional republic.

I look forward to sharing in an administration in which a President will entrust his Vice-President with vital responsibilities for the great problems of the states and the cities. For I have a strong belief that changes must be made and that the Nixon administration will make those changes.

I know, I am positive, that there is a better way to balance the complex relationship between federal, state, and local government than is presently being exercised. I know that the federal government must work more constructively, more creatively, and above all more simply in meeting the problems of prejudice and poverty in our cities.

I know there is a bright new world of ideas for cities such as cultural-commercial-industrial centers and satellite cities that we are only beginning to explore.

I know that America is reaching for the frontiers of space, and I am for it. But I also know we must treat generously the old, the sick, and the poor. We must help build independence and pride in the black community and make black Americans partners in our system.

I also know that more important than words in this campaign and in the next administration will be action, the kind of action that flows from involvement in the problems, and from the closest kind of relationship with the people who are involved in the problems. . . .

Now I want to assure you of one thing. As a political animal and a relatively sensitive individual who hopes he will never lose his sensitivity, I am not unaware of what took place in this convention hall tonight. I am aware that the reasons that motivated it were not directed at me in any personal sense and were merely responsive of the opinions of those that took part in the nomination of that great governor of Michigan, whom I consider my personal friend, Governor Romney. Those motives were simply to provide the strongest ticket for the Republican party in November.

I also recognize that a Vice-Presidential nominee does not come to the successful fruition of his nomination by virtue of his personality or his attractiveness or his ability to generate a wave of enthusiasm on his own. He comes here because he is the selection of the man who does all those things on his own, the Presidential nominee. I am privileged that that great future President of the United States, Richard M. Nixon, has seen fit to invest in me his confidence to do the job. But I will not be satisfied, ladies and gentlemen, I will not be satisfied under any circumstances, until I prove to you that I am capable of doing a job for the Republican party and the American people in November. . . .

He met the next morning with reporters, unhappy about what he had heard and read. He was "concerned about the first impression literally millions of Americans are getting about me." He could not, however, resist a slap at some of his liberal ex-friends. Even if his entire civil-rights record—which he considered a good one—had been made public, he said, it would not have changed some who were not willing to be impressed.

(Indeed, Agnew's civil-rights record had been a good one. State Senator Clarence Mitchell, Jr., son of the NAACP's Washington Director, said of his first few months in office: "He did more in moving in the direction of bettering black-white relations than any governor in the state's history."

In addition to naming Dr. Ware his supervisor for welfare programs and in pushing through a public accommodations bill, Agnew had removed the chairman of the Board of Electrical Examiners whom Negroes accused of bias, issued a statewide code of fair employment practices applying to state jobs and to firms doing business with the state, within months named a Negro, Judge Harry Cole, to the supreme bench of Baltimore city (he later named another and then a third Negro judge to the Baltimore municipal bench), endorsed black capitalism, called for "total open housing" and signed a bill prohibiting racial discrimination in the sale or rental of housing having more than five units, backed repeal of the state's antiquated miscegenation law, and appointed black men—the first in Maryland—to the State Workmen's Compensation Commission and to the Board of Engineering Examiners.

All this, however, was outweighed by the humiliation he caused Negro leaders in his public tongue-lashing during the Baltimore riots, a castigation that had been televised. Juanita Mitchell, Senator Mitchell's mother, later said Agnew had "no sensitivity" and rated property rights above human rights. Even Dr. Ware, now back in Washington, refers to his service in the Agnew administration as a "charade.")

As he spoke to reporters the morning after his nomination, Agnew remarked that he was "deeply disturbed it is being made to appear I'm to the right of King Lear."

Was Lear a rightist? a reporter asked.

Agnew's sense of humor took over. "Well," he mused, "he reserved unto himself the right to behead people, and, by my definition, that's a rightist's position."

Mrs. Agnew had called all the friends and relatives she could, except Randy in Vietnam.

Only Kim was unmoved. "Is that so?" she yawned when her mother reached her at Ocean City.

The morning after their nominations, Nixon and Agnew had their traditional breakfast with members of the Republican National Committee. Nixon was going to his vacation home at Key Biscayne, and asked Agnew to go with him. At Thompson's urging, because he was such a stranger to the press, Agnew decided to stay in Miami Beach. He spent most of the day giving interviews.

With a stop at the LBJ ranch in Texas, they flew the next day on Nixon's private plane to San Diego. Herb Thompson, Art Sohmer, Charles Bressler, Mrs. Agnew and the three girls were along. Kim was still bored.

At the ranch, still President Lyndon B. Johnson had summoned Secretary of State Dean Rusk, CIA Head Richard Helms and Cyrus Vance, our number-two delegate at the Paris Peace talks, to brief them. Johnson promised he would keep them minutely advised on developments in Vietnam throughout the campaign, a promise he kept.

The Agnew party stayed in California for a week before returning to Annapolis.

Reaction to Agnew's nomination among some Negro groups was predictable. Maryland Negro leaders pledged to work for his defeat. Philip Savage, director of the National Association for the Advancement of Colored People in Pennsylvania, said the Republicans "will not get a significant black vote in November." He charged Agnew's record in civil rights was "an unprogressive one. This man is totally out of step with the present needs of our cities."

The campaign got under way almost immediately. Agnew announced that he felt confident in turning the day-to-day conduct of state affairs over to his aides; that he would reserve to himself the right to make all policy decisions. He was promptly sued by two Maryland Democrats who claimed he was violating the Constitution. The courts held in his favor.

His schedule was controlled by Nixon's New York planning office. Vice-Presidential nominees travel back roads, anyhow. The news they make is largely local. They work harder—harder, in fact, than the top man on their tickets—but on the trunk wires, and in the larger dailies, what they say and do in Rochester, or Savannah, or Tucson, usually rates a couple of paragraphs tacked onto a major story.

Agnew campaigned in an American Airlines charter plane, a Boeing 727 he had named the *Michelle Ann*, after his only granddaughter. It had been altered to fit his needs. Rented electric typewriters were there for staff use. Telephones were installed in the aft section for newsmen, or for staffers to reach Nixon-Agnew headquarters in New York. Two compartments were built up front, one for the governor, his wife and daughters, his staff, and part of the twenty-five-man Secret Service unit who had been his constant companions since his nomination. (Security has been strict since the assassination of Senator Robert F. Kennedy. Even George Wallace and Curtis LeMay were being protected.)

But it was still whistle-stopping, even if no longer by rail. And Agnew learned as he went along: he learned to work the fences, behind which the crowd stood extending their hands, going hand over hand to avoid bruising one hand with constant use and to reach more people.

In a typical city, he had two hours and a half. Agnew was an agonizer about time; he stuck to his schedule. In two and one-half hours he'd banter with local politicians, greet the crowds at the airport, shake their hands, travel downtown, listen to plugs for local candidates, say something with a local angle, give local radio and television interviews. Then on to the next town.

Occasionally, his schedule was thrown out of whack. A too-long, too-windy introduction of local candidates, and he cut his remarks short. In his formal speeches, Mrs. Agnew, Pam, and Susan all sat on the platform, staring straight ahead. They didn't applaud when he was introduced or when the audience cheered him. "It would be like clapping for myself," Mrs. Agnew said. When he spoke in the open, from a flat-bed truck, from the foot of a war memorial, or from the steps of a courhouse, his Secret Service agents and local police were a few yards away, men with bulges on their hips, eyes sweeping the crowd. Agnew was guarded every sleeping and waking minute.

Between hops, aides dashed back and forth with clippings and memos on local events and people at the next stop, mention of which might get him votes.

Agnew had his own style. He didn't wade into crowds as the Kennedys did. He didn't pause for long conversations as

Senator Kennedy liked to do. The chatter was light. He must be able to meet the most people in the shortest period of time. Walking tours were not his style. He tried to hit the high spots.

Campaigning on the national level, he said, isn't much of a switch. Reverting to his Army days, he explains: "After a guy makes corporal, all other promotions are nothing by comparison."

Agnew made corporal when he was elected Baltimore County executive.

In the evenings he relaxed with a Scotch and soda, but was up early the next morning to resume his tour, unnoted by most of the nation, bringing the campaign to those who otherwise would be missed. It was the same with his Democratic opponent, Senator Edmund Muskie of Maine.

But with Agnew it was a little different. Already he had acquired a reputation for blunt speech, for sticking his foot in his mouth. He could be needled, he was new to the game, and he could be tricked. He was traveling with some real trap baiters. They were looking for ways to improve on an otherwise dull story.

In the 1952 campaign, Democrats concentrated on Richard Nixon, Dwight D. Eisenhower's running mate. With the disclosure of his "secret" campaign expense fund, the Nixon campaign train, then in Oregon, had the spotlight turned on it. Agnew was fair game, too.

(Agnew had, in fact, his own campaign-fund secret. Created after his election as governor, it was called the "Executive Assembly." Memberships were sold to prominent Republican businessmen for $1,000 each. It came to light when Agnew hosted a cocktail party at the governor's mansion for its contributor-members and statehouse reporters were denied admittance. Since approximately 150 guests were present, most stories said $150,000 had been raised. George White denies this. He said it never had more than $25,000, that its books were regularly audited, and that the money carefully was spent only for the governor's Republican party activities . . . "for instance, if he and his staff were to attend a Republican Governors' Conference it would come out of the fund." The "assembly" was disbanded after his nomination for Vice President.)

In the campaign, Agnew blooped occasionally.

Vice-President Hubert Humphrey, the Democratic nominee, had charged that Nixon was a "hardliner." Agnew retorted that Humphrey was "squishy soft" on Communism. There was an outcry. Agnew was accused of Joe McCarthyism.

In Rochester, New York, he was apologetic. He would, he said, "have turned five somersaults" to avoid using the term if he had known what interpretation would be placed on it.

"If I knew the phrase would relate in some way to cast me as the Joe McCarthy of 1968, I would have shunned it like the plague," he said.

Among others, the late Senator Everett Dirksen called to urge him to be more careful. There were reports that Nixon headquarters would send someone to ride herd on him.

(Ironically, back in Towson Agnew is still something of a villain to the John Birch Society, which peddles pamphlets with titles like *A Hard Look at Richard M. Nixon, The Romney Riddle, The Truth about Urban Development,* from an American Opinion bookstore a block from the courthouse.)

He was later accused of slurs on racial minorities. He had, it was reported, called a reporter aboard his campaign plane a "fat Jap." He had referred condescendingly to "Polacks," and he had said, "When you've seen one slum, you've seen them all."

Agnew kept his sense of humor. Asked by a television reporter to make his boners earlier in the day so that he could get them on the evening shows, the governor promised instead to spread them out, not to make them all in one week.

The reference to "Polacks" came in Chicago. Agnew was asked if he intended to visit the Negro slums. He replied that he did not think of a city in those terms, that no part of Chicago, as far as he was concerned, was Chinese, or Irish, or Polack, or Negro. Most of the reports missed it. But the *Washington Post* man did not. The story ran the next morning, and Agnew stood accused of ethnic bias.

The "fat Jap" incident came at the start of a flight on the *Michelle Ann* from Las Vegas to Los Angeles.

Gene Oishi of the *Baltimore Sun*, a Japanese married to a Swiss girl and a top-rate reporter who had covered the statehouse in Annapolis, had been out on the town the night before. He was aboard when the governor's party arrived, conked out asleep in his seat.

Agnew stopped and, amused, asked: "What's the matter with the fat Jap?"

Oishi awoke and they exchanged "good mornings." Agnew went on to the forward part of the plane.

Richard Homan, of the *Washington Post*, was seated next to Oishi. "Did you hear what he called you," Homan asked.

Still half-asleep, Oishi said he hadn't.

"He called you a 'fat Jap.' What are you going to say to that?"

Oishi laughed. "I call him a 'squishy-soft Greek,'" he said (a reference to the allusion to Humphrey for which Agnew had apologized), and went back to sleep.

Homan brought out his portable typewriter and wrote a mock press release about the incident. It circulated among the press and finally reached Agnew in the front of the plane. He laughed and wrote across it in ink, "If the fat Jap would lay off those TV dinners, he'd become a flat Jap."

Until now all this was good clean horseplay, the kind indulged in by reporters bored stiff with each other's enforced company and with writing essentially the same story day after day, night after night, wishing they were home with their families.

When they reached San Francisco, however, the man from *Time* approached Oishi and said he was writing a column about the amusing things that had happened on the Agnew plane. He wanted to use the fat Jap story.

Oishi asked him not to. He said it would embarrass him and Agnew and, moreover, would blow the story out of all proportions. The *Time* man came back the next day and repeated his request. He was desperate for a story of any kind. It was hard for one reporter to turn down another. Oishi told him to go ahead, but to leave out his name and the name of his newspaper.

Time did not use the story. But Homan had heard, and he asked if he might use it, too. Having agreed once, Oishi agreed again—on the same conditions.

By chance the story was picked up by the wire services about the same time Agnew's party reached Hawaii. On the floor of the House, Representative Sparks Matsanuga, a Democrat from Hawaii and one of the two Japanese-Americans in Congress, delivered an impassioned speech accusing Agnew of insulting his people.

At a stop on the island of Maui, Agnew felt compelled

once again to apologize. He did, mentioning Oishi and the *Sun* by name. Terribly embarrassed, Oishi was forced to write a story about himself and his newspaper.

Agnew had learned of Congressman Matsanuga's speech from reporters who met his plane at Honolulu.

He still regarded the incident as a vicious smear and believed that it had been deliberately set up to embarrass him.

When the plane reached Hilo, the next stop, Agnew invited the press up to his suite for cocktails. He was still visibly upset.

Bob Clark, of ABC, stood up and reproached other reporters for their behavior. He said he had been with the late Senator Robert Kennedy's campaign party and had heard the senator tell an offensive joke about Negroes. That story had never been published. He said Agnew was entitled to the same consideration.

The discussion became heated. Clark was the only man to defend Agnew; the Vice-President has been grateful to him ever since. Clark recalls that Homer Bigart of *The New York Times* made a "balanced and rational" defense of publishing the "fat Jap" story, but describes the rest of the press party as "young activists" out to gut Agnew at all costs. Clark argued heatedly that it was unethical to abuse the intimacy they shared on the campaign plane by publishing what was said in jest or in private conversation.

VII

A TARGET

In the closing days of the campaign, Towson found itself swarming with investigators and reporters.

They overflowed its two larger motels—the Park Towson and the Holiday Inn—and some of the smaller ones off the beltway. They came from many of the nation's major dailies and news magazines, and from the Democratic National Committee.

Towson resented them. It resented their leafing through

the dusty files in the courthouse. It resented the questions they asked. But it kept its temper.

Spiro T. Agnew, candidate for Vice-President on the Republican ticket, had become a target. Hopefully, he was Richard Nixon's Achilles heel. He had been hastily selected, and there had to be something he wanted to hide, some skeleton in his political closet.

For one thing, Spiro Agnew was new to the political scene, too new to have undergone the combing and going-over that older, more mature, politicians had. For another, he was from Maryland, a state of easygoing political ethics, where a number of high-ranking politicians, including a speaker of the state assembly elected from Baltimore County, had gone to prison.

Eight years before, Agnew had been all but penniless, working in a grocery store. Now, by his own public declaration, he had a net worth of $111,084, which included a $49,000 apartment in the Virgin Islands. Moreover, he had served on the county board of zoning appeals in the fifteen years that the county had grown from a population of 270,-000 to more than 500,000, and this growth had been accompanied by a corresponding boom in real estate values.

Spiro Agnew knew he was being checked. Little went on in Towson or Baltimore that did not reach his ear. He said he was "like Caesar's wife, above suspicion." He said he even reported as personal income the food bought for his family at the governor's mansion in Annapolis, although the state annually appropriates $20,000 to maintain and supply it.

Most of the snoopers were on fishing expeditions, looking for anything they could find. Little that they were unable to unearth was new; all of it had been aired in print and public statements by Agnew and his political enemies in the past.

These included:

● A charge by Charles Steinbock, Jr., an accountant and a Republican who was a candidate to succeed Agnew as county executive, that Agnew had tried to influence his decision as a member of the board of zoning appeals in favor of an Agnew client. Steinbock says Agnew asked him to "grant the position" and had his former law partner call to ask a favorable ruling "for the good of the Republican party."

Agnew said the charge was false and had "upset my family." He said he gave up the practice of law while county executive, but that a former client was pressing him for a

ruling so he called Steinbock and asked him only to acceler-
ate a decision. He said he "at no time suggested how he
should decide it."

• A charge that Agnew and eight close friends, all of
them wealthy businessmen, had shared in an investment in a
106-acre tract of land on the probable approach route to a
new span of the Chesapeake Bay Bridge, the state-owned toll
bridge near Annapolis. Among them were four who dealt
directly with the Baltimore County government. Agnew's
share was $34,200.

Agnew disclosed his part ownership in the land before he
was elected governor and said he would sell it, with any
profit to go to a children's home in Baltimore. It was sold at
public auction for $34,200, the exact amount Mr. Agnew had
paid. Thus, there was no profit. The buyer was Judge Harry
D. Blair, Jr., of the Maryland tax court, an Agnew ap-
pointee, representing the other eight investors.

• A charge that Agnew had been since 1964 a director of
the Chesapeake National Bank, which called itself the only
locally owned bank in Towson, although 51 percent of its
stock is owned by Financial General Corporation of Washington, D.C. Agnew was charged with a conflict of interest
because the county government deposited funds in the bank
while he was executive, and because it was also a depository
for state money.

Agnew had disclosed his ownership of bank stock and his
directorship in the resolution by the county council authoriz-
ing deposit of funds there. He owned 400 shares, worth
approximately $11,000.

Agnew replied that the state does not have an account at
Chesapeake National Bank, except for a $200,000 certificate
of deposit purchased by the state treasurer, John Leutkemeyer, a Democrat, under Governor J. Millard Tawes.

• A charge that Agnew had falsely stated that he had
inherited the bank stock from his father when, in fact, his
father had died a year before it was opened. Agnew denied
this. He said he had explained that his father had left him
stock worth $10,000 in a creamery and that he had sold it,
then bought bank stock.

• A charge that Agnew had invested in a Virgin Islands
land venture. He admitted he had put $1,600 in a condomini-
um that had thus far shown a loss, and that later he had

bought a vacation apartment in the same project for $49,-000.

This close scrutiny might have gone unnoticed by everyone except Agnew and his friends in Towson had not *The New York Times* charged in an editorial that his business dealings represented a "clear and repeated conflict of interest" which showed he was "not fit to stand one step away from the Presidency." *indirect, subtle, and derogatory implication*

Now, by innuendo, Agnew stood accused not only as a racist, and unthinking clod spewing ethnic epithets, but also as some sort of scoundrel. *a term used to characteriz the nature of a person or thing.*

He was indignant—angry.

From Houston, where he was campaigning, he lashed back: *feeling or expressing anger.*

It is unfortunate that *The New York Times,* long considered one of the leading publications in this country, should find itself in the embarrassing position of having pulled the major blooper of this campaign.

Everyone knows that *The Times* endorsed Vice-President Humphrey and is actively supporting him. The fact that *The Times* waited until a week before the election to distort the facts and make its inaccurate charges against me compounds this libel.

Before this editorial was written *The Times* was advised by my campaign manager that its information was inaccurate. Specifically, *The Times* charged, or inferred, that because of the favorable treatment given friends of mine while I was in office, my financial worth had "risen sharply." This is a completely false statement. No improper treatment was given friends of mine while I was in office. Moreover, if you eliminate some $35,000 to $40,000 that I inherited or was given by my parents, my net worth is considerably less than that of the other Presidential or Vice-Presidential candidates. My total net worth is $111,084.44. Eliminating the monies received from my parents, my net worth would be $74,000.

Agnew dealt in detail with the charges of financial chicanery on his part. He pointed out that Chesapeake National is a national and not a state bank. He denied that he had ever deposited any county money in the bank while he was Baltimore County executive. Such decisions, he said, are made by the county director of finance, whose recommendations he followed.

> The Times has stated that if it finds its editorial to be inaccurate, it will write a retraction in its editorial columns. There is documentary proof of what I say and I assume The Times will keep its word [he said].

Unfortunately, when someone is libeled in this fashion, a retraction does not reach all the persons who read the original libel. In addition, other newspapers and other news media pick up the original libel and repeat it before the retraction appears, thus compounding the situation.

The reporter [Ben A. Franklin] who made the investigation for The Times reported to it that all the above charges were old allegations and that his investigation "turned up little hard fact that is new."

The Times knew of these old charges and had a complete file on me in 1966 when it endorsed me for governor of Maryland, and I quote two of its statements:

> "As executive of Baltimore County, Agnew has gained the experience to be a competent governor."

> "Both the state of Maryland and the cause of modern-minded Republicans in the nation will benefit if the voters elect him."

The Times's reply was to reprint its editorial.

John B. Mitchell, Nixon's campaign manager who would become his attorney general, called The Times article a "distortion of the true facts." George White, Agnew's campaign manager, deplored its "wanton, reckless disregard for the rights and reputation of others. The Times has become so powerful and arrogant it thinks it can do as it pleases. A newspaper is supposed to fairly and impartially report the news. The Times has violated this code of ethics . . . lost all sense of decency." The general counsel for the Chesapeake National Bank asked for a retraction. He said Agnew "has avoided conflict of interest in his dealings with the bank and its directors" and said the charges "seriously affect the National Banking Association and reflects on the personal integrity of its officers and board."

By any standard, George White was an unusual choice for campaign manager by a Vice-Presidential candidate.

A small-town lawyer, he had never held political office and

says now he does not want one. He had met Ted Agnew when Agnew first came to Towson twenty years before, and they shared office space and a single stenographer—though they were not formally partners—at 24 West Pennsylvania Sreet, two blocks from the courthouse.

When Agnew, as Baltimore County executive, first thought about running for governor, he went to White and asked for his support. White says he gave it on the spot, but added, "And I hope you lose, so you can get back to the practice of law."

His only early contribution, he recalls, was to lend Agnew his white convertible so he and Judy could take part in a Fourth of July parade when Agnew was running for county executive—"that's how hard up he was, and how he got around then."

White now recalls that he and Agnew were in San Francisco when he received a long-distance call from *The Times* reporter, Ben Franklin. Franklin had been with the Agnew campaign off and on; he and Agnew got along well, White remembers. White said Franklin said he had to talk with him (White), but did not want to discuss the matter over the phone.

They met when Agnew's party returned to Washington. White says Franklin's first remark was: "I'm afraid your campaign is in real trouble."

Franklin said, White recalls, that Towson was swarming with investigators, all trying to get something on Agnew. He recalls specifically that Franklin mentioned the *Washington Post* and the *Baltimore Sun*. Franklin said he had also investigated Agnew, because he had to protect his newspaper and if there was something on the Vice-Presidential candidate he wanted to know what it was. White said Franklin also had investigated him (White).

White asked what in particular they were checking.

He said Franklin replied that there was "some talk of a payoff" in connection with Agnew's veto of a generic drug bill while he was governor. He said he had been unable to find anything, in fact, that most of the material he had dug up was old, and he intended to write that he had found Agnew was an "honest man."

White expressed doubt *The Times* would print such a story. Franklin, however, wrote it and it was carried.

The generic drug bill had been sponsored by Assemblyman

Walter Orlinsky, a Baltimore Democrat, and would have required the state to use less expensive generic drugs, rather than name brands, in its state and federally aided programs. Agnew had, at first, been for it. Later, after a briefing by the state medical association and major drug manufacturers, he agreed to veto it. Agnew admitted at the time he did not feel qualified as a layman to pass on the matter.

Franklin said those checking Agnew's record were also interested in his bank directorship and the bridge land deal.

Franklin's recollections do not differ substantially from White's.

He said their conference in White's suite at the Shoreham Hotel in Washington lasted only about forty-five minutes. Agnew sat in for approximately thirty minutes and became increasingly annoyed, Franklin said, not because of the substance of any of the charges against him, but because they were all old and were being dredged up again. He said he told White it was "proper" for Agnew to be investigated because he had been so recently propelled into the national limelight. He said he told White he and, as far as he knew, other reporters had not turned up anything new on Agnew.

John B. Oakes, head of *The Times*'s editorial board, said the editorial criticizing Agnew was "a moderately worded expression of some of the reasons for *The Times* belief that Mr. Agnew is unfit to be Vice-President of the United States."

Agnew's stongest defender turned out to be Richard M. Nixon.

Nixon had not forgotten the loneliness he knew in 1952 when General Eisenhower seemed to all but abandon him in the controversy swirling around his secret campaign fund, and leave him to sink or swim.

He was determined that would not happen to *his* running mate.

Appearing on national television, he angrily denied that Agnew's interest in the Chesapeake National Bank conflicted with his duties when he was a county official or governor of Maryland.

"This is the lowest kind of gutter politics that a great newspaper could possibly engage in," Nixon said. "These changes are stale. They were made two years ago. They were answered then."

Nixon said a retraction would be demanded "legally."

Oakes replied that Nixon "denies no statement of fact in the editorial except one on which he is quite imprecise. As soon as we know exactly which one of Mr. Agnew's conflicts of interest it is that Mr. Nixon challenges, we will, of course, reinvestigate. If any statement of ours should prove to be in error, we will say so on the editorial page."

The day after Nixon said a legal retraction would be demanded, White went to New York to meet with Harding Bancroft, a *Times* executive. White demanded a retraction; Bancroft refused. White argues that while libel laws now permit newspapers to "say almost anything" about a public figure, if one prints libel knowing at the time the story is false, it is liable to damages. He said *The Times* knew the story was false, because Franklin had told its editors so.

Why didn't Agnew sue?

"A week later, he was elected," White says. "The Vice-President of the United States can't be going around suing newspapers for libel.

Meanwhile, the Republicans were beginning to worry that Nixon and Agnew had peaked too early. Humphrey, who seemed at first not to get going, indeed student militants often would not let him speak, seemed to have caught on. The polls showed him gaining. He played the role of under-dog well, and he played it to the hilt. There was something engaging about Humphrey. Nixon and Agnew, on the other hand, often seemed to lack warmth.

A week before the election, most polls showed Humphrey five to eight percentage points behind—and gaining.

They waited for Nixon to crack, as he had done in the past, but this time he fooled them. Boarding a jet for another leg of his campaign tour at New York City, he showed no sign of concern as he bantered with newsmen. He seemed jaunty, confident, and optimistic.

"Put this down as a flat prediction," he said, slapping his hands together for emphasis. ". . . I predict I will run three percent better than [George] Gallup and five percent better than [Louis] Harris."

George White credits the flap over *The New York Times* editorials with turning the tide and helping elect Nixon-Agnew. He says it was the turning point of the campaign.

Immediately, he recalls, the *Washington Post,* the *Baltimore Sun,* and the *St. Louis Globe Democrat* disassociated themselves from the attack. The *Sun* and *Post-Dispatch*, he says, "were particularly hard on the Old Gray Lady." Most of Maryland's elected Democratic officials came to Agnew's defense, including his old foe, State Comptroller Goldstein. John Leutkemeyer, the Democratic state treasurer, went on television to denounce *The New York Times* and to vouch for Agnew as an honest man.

Agnew was still campaigning when the time came for him to go back to Annapolis and wait for the results.

The next morning he was Vice-President-elect of the United States. Nixon-Agnew had run up an impressive 302 electoral votes. Humphrey-Muskie had 191, and Wallace-LeMay had 45. The popular vote was much closer. Nixon-Agnew had 31,304,992, Humphrey-Muskie scored 30,994,-354, and Wallace-LeMay had 9,825,459.

Again, only twelve-year-old Kim was unimpressed. "I don't like moving," she told reporters.

VIII

VICE-PRESIDENT

The Vice-President of the United States shall be the President of the Senate, but shall have no vote unless they are equally divided. —Article I, Section 3, Constitution of the United States.

In case of the removal of the President from office, or of his death, resignation or inability to discharge the powers and duties of said office, the same shall devolve on the Vice-President. —Article II, Section 2.

Thus, the Constitution makes the office Spiro Agnew had been elected to fill at once the most impotent and the most potentially powerful in the United States.

John Adams, our first Vice-President, called his job "the most insignificant office that ever the invention of man contrived or his imagination conceived."

Woodrow Wilson believed its importance was that the Vice-President "may cease to be Vice-President."

Daniel Webster was offered the nomination in 1848 and refused. "I do not propose to be buried until I am really dead," he said.

Thomas R. Marshall told a parable about the office: Once there were two brothers. One ran away to sea, the other was elected Vice-President, and nothing was ever heard of either of them again.

During the nineteenth century, it was not unusual for the Vice-President to live and work in his home state and commute to Washington when the Senate was in session. Nor was it unusual for a Presidential candidate not to know his Vice-Presidential nominee. Lincoln met both his future Vice-Presidents, Hannibal Hamlin and Andrew Johnson, after they were nominated by the Republican conventions.

Yet men eagerly seek the second spot on major party tickets. Lyndon B. Johnson was half-convinced that Senator Eugene McCarthy's opposition to him stemmed from the fact he was passed over in favor of a fellow Minnesotan, Hubert Humphrey, in 1964. Some even campaign for it—as Governor John Volpe of Massachusetts did at Miami Beach—though in recent years a political party's Presidential nominee has had the right to pick his running mate. The only exception was when the late Adlai Stevenson, nominated to oppose President Eisenhower for the second time in 1956, threw the Democratic race open and made no choice. The near-thing race between the late President John F. Kennedy, then junior senator from Massachusetts, and the late Senator Estes Kefauver of Tennessee—which Kefauver won—catapulted Kennedy into his nomination and election as President four years later.

In the early days of the Republic, the high man in the Electoral College became President, the runner-up became his Vice-President. The only condition was that they must not come from the same state. Thus, in 1797 we had John Adams, champion of the hateful Alien and Sedition Act, as President, and Thomas Jefferson, civil-libertarian, author of the Declaration of Independence, champion of a free press, as his second-in-command.

Jefferson's Vice-President was Aaron Burr, a man he regarded as a scoundrel. Jefferson and Burr each had 63 electoral votes, and Alexander Hamilton engineered Jefferson's eventual victory. Burr later killed Hamilton in a duel. He was charged with murder, but never brought to trial.

In 1804, the twelfth amendment to the Constitution put an end to the runner-up system and Jefferson was reelected with his own man, George Clinton, former governor of New York.

Who have been our Vice-Presidents, the men Benjamin Franklin once called "our superfluous excellencies"?

Some have succeeded to the Presidency and become better known than others. The Vice-President is always one heartbeat away from the highest office in the land.

First to move up was Millard Fillmore, a man who had failed to get elected governor of his home state, New York. When his President, Zachary Taylor, died in office, Fillmore split the Whip party with his support of a program Taylor opposed.

John Tyler, who succeeded President William Henry Harrison after a month, was later elected to the Confederate Congress from Virginia, but approaching death kept him from taking his seat.

Chester A. Arthur succeeded President James A. Garfield and lived down his reputation as an unsavory spoilsman. He sponsored the civil service.

Andrew Johnson, an illiterate Tennesseean who learned to read and write after his marriage, narrowly escaped impeachment when he tried to carry out Lincoln's policies toward the conquered South. His enemies said he was a drunk.

Theodore Roosevelt succeeded William McKinley after his assassination, later was elected President, and then split with the party to run for President on the Bull Moose ticket. Fillmore, Martin Van Buren, and Henry A. Wallace, among former Veeps, also ran later on splinter tickets.

Teddy was even more outspoken than Agnew, though, apparently, commentators were less squeamish in his day.

"Professional pacifists," he once said, "should be regarded as traitors to the great casue of justice and humanity."

"The voice of the weakling or the craven," he said on another occasion, "counts for nothing when he clamors for peace."

He also said, "Only those are fit to live who do not fear to die; and none are fit to die who have shrunk from the joy of life and the duty of life"; and "A pacifist is as surely a traitor to his country and to humanity as the most brutal wrongdoer."

Calvin Coolidge succeeded Warren G. Harding. He had been chosen for his firmness in putting down a Boston police strike while governor of Massachusetts. As President he was a man of few words—"What was the sermon about? Sin. What did the preacher say about sin? He was against it." Coolidge finished Harding's term, was elected to another at the end of which he did not choose to run again.

Harry Truman took the torch from the fallen Franklin D. Roosevelt in time to drop the atomic bomb on Japan. Lyndon Johnson inherited Vietnam from John Kennedy.

If we remember our Vice-Presidents at all, it usually is for other things.

Marshall (Woodrow Willson) wanted a good five-cent cigar for his country.

Charles G. Dawes (Calvin Coolidge) was barely on speaking terms with the White House. He refused to attend Cabinet meetings because he believed the Vice-President did not belong there. Dawes smoked a pipe unside down.

Old-timers remember Herbert Hoover's Vice-President, Charles Curtis of Kansas, because his sister, Dolly Gann, became embroiled in a bitter feud with Alice Roosevelt Longworth, Teddy's daughter, over who was Washington's top hostess.

Vice-President-elect Agnew waited until the last minute to give up the governorship of Maryland while Democrats fumed and jockeyed for position to succeed him. He left with a nostalgic summary of his accomplishments and headed down Route 50 to Washington, thirty miles away. Assembly Speaker Marvin Mandel; a Democrat from Baltimore city, was chosen to succeed him.

Washington brought changes in their lives. For years, there has been talk in Washington of building an official residence for the Vice-President. Nothing has ever come of it. The most oft-mentioned site is Observatory Hill, on Massachusetts Avenue NW, near Embassy Row, where the incumbent chief of naval operations has his quarters.

Spiro Agnew, like his predecessors, had to look for a place to live. He and Mrs. Agnew picked a nine-room apartment in the Sheraton Park Hotel which, reportedly, cost them $1,500 a month—"I'm afraid to ask," Mrs. Agnew told reporters. But his salary was soon raised from $43,000 a year to $62,500 a year. Mrs. Agnew acquired her first mink coat, a clothing consultant to coordinate her wardrobe, a secretary to handle her mail and one to deal with the press, and her own Secret Service detail.

Nixon had been Vice-President and lived for eight years in Eisenhower's bigger-than-life shadow. He gave the Vice-President an office in the White House—a first—for his modest staff. Agnew had a chauffeured limousine, an office near the Senate Chamber on Capitol Hill, an official frank for mailing purposes, and his own flag and seal.

In the past four decades, the Vice-Presidency has gradually emerged from a passive office to active participation in day-to-day executive operations.

Vice-President John Nance Garner met with President Franklin D. Roosevelt's Cabinet as a matter of course until they fell out politically and Garner went back to Texas.

During the Second World War, Vice-President Henry Wallace, who succeeded Garner, was chairman of the Board of Economic Warfare, and in 1941 was named to the Presidential Advisory Committee on the Development and Use of Atomic Energy.

Nixon was chairman of President Eisenhower's Committee on Governmental Contracts and his personal representative in party affairs, which bored and mystified the old general. Johnson was chairman of Kennedy's Committee on Equal Opportunity. Humphrey served as Johnson's liaison with local governments.

Yet a President is, by nature of the fact that he is a President, an individualist. Vice-Presidents, by the nature of their jobs, are overshadowed by Presidents. Hubert Humphrey once defined the office: "The Vice-President is, and is what, the President wants him to be ... a loyal, faithful friend and servant."

This was the job to which Governor Agnew succeeded, heir to a long line of "superfluous excellencies." His job would be what Richard Nixon wanted it to be, no more, no less.

Few Presidents have used their Vice-Presidents as skillfully as Nixon has. The explanation may lie in his long apprenticeship, his intense study of the office of President and its potential. It is not that Agnew has become an Assistant President; he hasn't. He is not a regular adviser on either domestic or foreign affairs, though he in consulted. He has been permitted, instead, to carve out his own niche, to seek his own level, build his own image.

Nixon has his own views on the Vice-Presidency. The job, he said, "is so important that it no longer can or should be used simply to balance a ticket geographically or ideologically. I want a man for Vice-President who, if something should happen to me, would make the best President of the United States . . . the Vice-Presidency has now become an important office in its own right. The Presidency is so big and its responsibilities in international affairs particularly are so great, that we need a Vice-President who can undertake great responsibilities and the President will trust."

As Agnew saw the job, "You must be prepared to step, at a moment's notice, into any area of government that the President designates."

In his acceptance speech at Miami Beach, Agnew had said he looked forward to working with a President who would "entrust his Vice-President with vital responsibilities for the great problems of the states and cities." Nixon delivered. He gave Agnew direct responsibility and control over the Office of Intergovernmental Relations—making him his contact man with the nation's governors and mayors. When the governors met in Colorado Springs, it was Vice-President Agnew who had to break the bad news there would be less federal money available to them for a while.

Nixon made the Vice-President chairman of the National Aeronautics and Space Council, the National Council on Marine Resources and Engineering Development, the President's Council on Youth Opportunity, the Peace Corps National Advisory Council, the President's Council on Physical Fitness and Sports, and the National Council on Indian Opportunity. By law, Agnew sits on the National Security Council, the Council on Urban Affairs, and the Environmental Quality Council, and presides in the President's absence.

Nixon has sent Agnew overseas. But other Presidents have done that. Jack Kennedy sent Lyndon Johnson on a world tour that wound up with his bringing a Pakistani camel driver back to Washington. Nixon toured South America for Eisenhower and was almost lynched in Caracas. Humphrey circled the globe for Johnson and was his stand-in at the funeral of the late Winston Churchill.

But few have gone better briefed, better informed, and entrusted to speak with greater authority than Spiro Agnew when he left for an eleven-nation tour of Southeast Asia in

December, 1969. Nixon sped him on his way to explain the new Nixon doctrine for Asia.

His sharpest critics—and God knows he still has them—had to admit he performed admirably. Headlined *The New York Times*: "Agnew: A Roving Envoy Comes on Strong." In fact, his skill at dodging pratfalls and in not stubbing his toe—as so many had expected—seemed an affront.

"The Vice-President, "*The Times* quoted an unidentified diplomat as saying, "is sticking right to the script."

In Manila, where he attended the inauguration of President Ferdinand Marcos, Agnew emphasized that the United States would keep its commitments to its allies and would, if necessary, use its total power to ward off any major threat to our friends in the Pacific.

What he said, however, was lost back home in more sensational reports of anti-American demonstrations. One wire service said a "bomb" was thrown at his limousine as it entered the American Embassy grounds in Manila. The *Washington Evening Star* was more restrained. It described the object as a firecracker.

As he plowed ahead on his man-killing schedule, breaking fresh ground, seeing new faces, Agnew grew more confident. He carefully remembered all the "dos" and "don'ts" of State Department advisers. At Singapore he told 200 cheering Americans that the Nixon doctrine "has struck a responsive note. We have found the understanding of the new American posture and a reassured feeling the United States in not going to turn its back on Asia."

Back home, Chairman J. William Fulbright (D.-Ark.) of the Senate Foreign Relations Committee, was moved to denounce Vice-President Agnew as a "smart aleck." Agnew, in Malaysia, said Fulbright "seems to have lost his cool." He offered to brief the acid-tongued Arkansawyer of foreign policy on his return "if he asks me."

Agnew felt he gained in understanding on his Asian tour. "The people back home don't understand as well as they might what's actually happening in Asian countries," he said. "I can say that because I didn't understand myself until this trip."

There continued to be anti-American demonstrations, and they were grist for the mills of the press. Americans led some of the protesters in Nepal, which has become some sort of hippie haven, and there were peace corpsmen in the crowds in Afghanistan. His treatment by a handful of young activists was roughest in Australia and New Zealand, though his reception was overwhelming cordial in both nations.

Agnew said mildly that the demonstrators were "rather childish in their deportment." Mrs. Agnew called them "frustrated cheerleaders."

His critics, of course, were not disposed to let him get away with a clean bill of health if they could help it and in an editorial on January 6, 1970, headed "The Things a Certain Vice-President Will Say" the *Washington Post* found his performance "confusing."

"It is enough to note one good reason for *not* sending Vice-Presidents on tour and that is the use of such ceremonial occasions as a forum for furthering vendettas with the critics back home," it lectured.

"A private talk with Prime Minister Kittikachorn in Bangkok seems somehow the wrong platform, as it were, for a statement that 'some people back home are so anxious to make friends of our enemies that they ever seem ready to make enemies of our friends.'"

The *Post's* sensibilities clearly were outraged.

"Aside from the fact that statement is too indiscriminate to be anything more than nasty in a general way, it is a little like going to Montgomery, Alabama, to attack *The New York Times* and *Washington Post*. Yet the Vice-President took pains to see that this particular portion of his private utterances to the prime minister was available to the press."

Agnew had stopped in Vietnam and had visited front-line troops while there.

"Don't be misled,"he told them, "by what you may see and read in certain publications. . . . The American people are darned proud of you and what you are doing . . . don't let anyone tell you that the people back home aren't with you, because they are, 100 percent."

"Some days," the *Post* said archly, "Mr. Agnew attacks the press by name and some days he doesn't, and we don't know whom he had in mind this time. What we do know is that once again he has it all wrong. The quarrel that 'some people' and 'certain publications' back home have with the Vietnam war has nothing to do, and never had anything to do, with the men in the field. . . . The quarrel is, and always has been, with the managers of this war, the military strategists and their civilian supervisors, the policymakers and the decisionmakers. People higher up like Cabinet members and Presidents—and even Vice-Presidents."

Whatever the *Post* might say, however, President Nixon told a news conference that Agnew's Asian tour was "an enormously effective trip from the standpoint of the United States . . . this was one of the most substantive trips ever taken by a Vice-President of the United States."

Nixon had always thought highly of Agnew. The decision to make him the party's Vice-Presidential nominee may have been close, but the two had used the months since their introduction by Louise Gore to become close associates, if not close friends.

"I know Ted Agnew well," the President wrote in Ann Pinchot's book *Spiro Agnew: Where He Stands*. "We have had long and tough discussions. We have examined each other's ideas, debated issues, and tested each other. He had real depth and genuine warmth. Having watched his performance as governor of Maryland, I was deeply impressed with his tremendous brainpower, great courage, and unprejudiced legal mind. He had vigor and imagination and, above all, he acts. Under pressure, he is poised and controlled. When it comes to carrying the ball and resisting the attack, he's got it."

At a gathering of Republican nationality groups at the White House in October, 1969, the President said: "I am very proud to have the Vice-President with his Greek background in this administration. He has done a fine job. . . ."

In a relatively short time, Spiro Agnew had gone from unknown to hairshirt to an asset to the Nixon administration. Now he was about to take his biggest step forward.

He was about to become a folk hero.

Agnew's views—widely and forcefully expressed—are very much his own. No statement could have been more forthright than his lecture to Maryland's Negro leaders during the riots of April, 1968. He showed real courage when he refused to back down in face of what was, to him then, certain knowledge he had committed political suicide.

Agnew's views stem from a deep-seated belief in traditional values and an even greater disappointment in many in this country who have failed to live up to them or rejected them entirely.

When Kim succumbed to the excitement of the hour and

wanted to join the Vietnam moratorium in October, 1969, he said "No."

"Parental-type power must be exercised," he said when the story broke in the newspapers. "Some parents have forgotten how."

Bill Raspberry, the *Washington Post*'s able Negro commentator, a liberal, applauded.

Writing in *The New York Times* on November 2, 1969, Robert B. Semple, Jr., said of Agnew: "As for his views, nobody knows a great deal." If so, one has not read the record. Ted Agnew's views are explicitly clear over a long period of time.

There has been a continuing debate whether or not he speaks for President Nixon. There is no evidence of it. Mr. Nixon insists he does not censor what his Vice-President says, or that he has advance knowledge of it. If they seem to speak with one voice, it is because they are very much on the same wavelength. Few among the two top men in our history have been more sharply attuned.

But Nixon, over the years, has learned to be careful in what he says, to speak only after mature reflection, to consider the impact of every word. Agnew will use the language he would use in talking with Judge Barrett in his own living room. What many deplore as simplistic nonsense, most Americans regard as common sense. And if Agnew speaks that language, it is not the result of a contrived conspiracy, but because he believes as they do.

Washington has a language of its own, as does New York. Ironically, while many in both cities profess to prefer plain speech—"Tell it like it is"—their horror at Agnew when he does must reveal something.

He had spoken many times before, but the Vice-President seemed to leap into the spotlight on the night of October 19, 1969, with an address at a citizen's testimonial dinner in New Orleans. It was here the term "effete snobs" was added to the nation's dictionary of catch phrases.

> . . . We seem to be approaching an age of the gross. Persuasion through speeches and books is too often discarded for disruptive demonstrations aimed at bludgeoning the unconvinced into action.
>
> The young—and I don't mean by any stretch of the imagination all the young, I'm talking about those who claim to

speak for the young—at the zenith of physical power and sensitivity, overwhelm themselves with drugs and artificial stimulants. Subtlety is lost, and fine distinctions based on acute reasoning are carelessly ignored in a headlong jump to a predetermined conclusion. Life is visceral rather than intellectual, and most visceral practitioners of life are those who characterize themselves intellectuals.

Truth to them is "revealed" rather than logically proved, and the principal infatuations of today revolve around the social sciences, those subjects which can accommodate any opinion and about which the most reckless conjecture cannot be discredited.

Education is being redefined at the demand of the uneducated to suit the ideas of the uneducated. The student now goes to college to proclaim rather than to learn. The lessons of the past are ignored or obliterated in a contemporary antagonism known as the generation gap. A spirit of national masochism prevails, encouraged by an effete corps of impudent snobs who characterize themselves as intellectuals.

That tore it. Wealthy, old Averill Harriman, who had traipsed around Washington proclaiming the merits of the North Vietnamese position since he lost his job in Paris, threw a Georgetown party and greeted guests at the door with "Welcome, effete snobs." Hippies started wearing lapel buttons proclaiming themselves "Effete Snobs for Peace."

It is in this setting of dangerous oversimplification that the war in Vietnam achieves its greatest distortion [Agnew continued].

The recent Vietnam Moratorium is a reflection of the confusion that exists in America today. Thousands of well-motivated young people, conditioned since childhood to respond to great emotional appeals, saw fit to demonstrate for peace. Most did not stop to consider that the leaders of the Moratorium had billed it as a massive public outpouring of sentiment against the foreign policy of the United States. Most did not care to be reminded that the leaders of the Moratorium refused to disassociate themselves from the objectives enunciated by the enemy in Hanoi.

If the Moratorium had any use whatever, it served as an emotional purgative for those who felt the need to cleanse themselves of their lack of ability to offer a constructive solution to the problem. . . .

. . . Great patriots of past generations would find it difficult to believe that Americans would ever doubt the validity of America's resolve to protect free men from totalitarian attack. Yet today, we see those among us who prefer to side with an enemy aggressor rather than stand by this free nation. We see others who are shortsighted enough to believe that we need not protect ourselves from attack by governments that depend upon force to control their people—governments which came into being through force alone and continue to exist by force alone.

I do not want to see this nation spend one dollar more on defense than is absolutely necessary, but I would hate to see this nation spend one dollar less on defense than is absolutely necessary. Until the principle of open representative government exists among all nations, the United States must not abandon its moral obligation to protect by any means necessary the freedoms so hard won by past generations, the freedoms so hard won by the 400,000 Americans who made the ultimate sacrifice in dedicated belief that some things are more precious than life itself.

The outcry was deafening. On scholarly panels, on television, and in the press each word was dissected and analyzed. No one could believe that Agnew meant exactly what he had said. Someone had put him up to it. What were his motives?

In November, *Time* characterized him as a "cartoon character called 'Suburbaman,' the yodel-type" and his wife whose "life revolved around their four kids and their home," and who preferred "family domestic life which, in years past, consisted largely of law sprinklers, pizza, pingpong in the basement rec room, Sunday afternoons watching the Baltimore Colts on color Television." Besides which, they hadn't joined the Washington social scene, preferring to enterain their old Maryland friends.

Clare Crawford leapt to the Agnews' defense. While "I have enjoyed Agnew jokes more than most," she wrote, "I also like pizza, old friends, Ocean City, lawn sprinklers, and my children. Frankly, I like Judy and Spiro Agnew. They are among the few real people in Washington. They are themselves and not caricatures of Washington party goers. They're alive—a rare quality in this subdued government."

Actually, the Vice-President had said pretty much the same thing before, and it had been widely overlooked. At commencement ceremonies at Ohio State University in Columbus on June 7 he had lashed out at "effetism."

Your generation [he had said then] is not the first youth who ever questioned the efficacy of a custodial generation. You are not the first to aggressively challenge the fundamental values of a society. Such challenges are normal, proper, and the basis for human improvement.

We are not in turmoil because of your testing. We are in trouble because my generation has apparently failed to define and defend either its achievements or its inheritance from past generations of Americans.

A society which fears its children is effete. A sniveling, hand-wringing power structure deserves the violent rebellion it encourages. If my generation doesn't stop cringing, yours will inherit a lawless society where emotion and muscle displace reason.

A society which looks calmly into the logic or illogic of its youth's anger and ambition, accepting the rational and rejecting the immature, is alive.

My purpose is not to castigate youth nor discuss where the generations differ. My purpose is to point out the case for American democracy and to challenge you to determine whether the advantages all Americans enjoy would have developed outside our free enterprise system.

. . . This nation was founded on two great concepts—liberty and equality of opportunity . . . Our Constitution—the world's oldest enduring document designed to create a free and open society—guarantees a government of laws not men. . . . The history of this nation is a lesson in the advantage of political freedom . . .

. . . All is not perfect. The purpose of our Constitution is not to promise perfection, but to establish a more perfect union. Happiness is not a universal condition among us. Our Constitution does not guarantee happiness. But ours is the only Constitution pledged to the "pursuit" of it. Our Constitution does not guarantee perpetual equality, but only the vigilant maintenance of the opportunity to be equal or excel.

Two centuries of a people's high dedication did not result

from rhetoric but recognition that this country does offer the best way of life.

Still later in that speech, he said:

> I have lived half a century. Perhaps our accomplishments during my lifetime furnish a reasonable test of progress. . . . I can remember when Charles Lindbergh landed his single-engined *Spirit of St. Louis* in Paris. Now, I look forward to America's lunar landing next month. The computer, the transitor, television, jet planes, radio astronomy, the laser, and nuclear energy were developments of the past fifty years.
>
> In the last twenty-five years alone, mankind has acquired more scientific knowledge than in all previous history. . . . Life expectancy has increased, infant mortality decreased. The dread diseases of polio, typhus, malaria, measles, smallpox, pellegra, and rabbies have been virtually eradicated. . . .
>
> We have a choice. Will we treat all that is wrong with America as a challenge or as an indictment? Will we attack our problems or just weep over them? Will we condemn our institutions or correct them? Will we repudiate democracy because it moves slowly, or revitalize it so its pace quickens?

Earlier, in Hawaii, he had made a passionate defense of what since has become known as the "silent majority."

> . . . America's ruling majority embraces many minorities. Many myths about the American majority are without substance.
>
> The ruling majority is neither all white, nor all affluent, nor all callous.
>
> The American majority may not be book-intellectual, but it is practical. It may not be passionately committed to any ideology, but it is passionately against intolerant dogmatism.
>
> Finally, the majority is bewildered by our present irrational protest.

The public responded enthusiastically. Republican governors made him their hero and asked him to help in their reelection campaigns. His name had, indeed, become a household word. At the Republican Governors' Conference in Hot Springs, Arkansas, in December, 1969, governor after governor said Agnew is "saying what the people want to hear."

Pennsylvania's Governor Raymond P. Shafer exulted: "Ted Agnew has become a big gun in the Republican political arsenal. He's going to be no end of help next year."

Governor Louie Nunn, of Kentucky, went further: "Popular in my state?" he asked. "Hell, yes. I'd say he's more popular right now than Richard Nixon."

Governor Cargo of New Mexico said Agnew is saying "exactly what the majority of the people in my state want to hear."

And with appropriate obeisance toward the White House, Kansas freshman Senator Robert Dole told Nixon: "Next to you, Mr. President, Vice-President Agnew is the one Republican who can get money for us without carrying a gun."

There were exceptions, of course. New York Senator Charles Goodell asked Agnew to stop his "inflammatory rhetoric" and "baseless charges" against the antiwar demonstrators. Agnew kept silent. Goodell, after all, was a Republican.

The Vice-President was deluged with invitations. He found himself avidly sought out by states where he would not have been entirely welcome a few months earlier. The polls showed him to have massive popular support.

Agnew was active lgeislatively, too. During the floor fight in the Senate over the anti-ballistic missile bases—when it looked for a while as though he might have to break a tie vote—his Senate office was a command post for the ABM forces. White House liaison Bryce Harlow worked out of it. Minority Leader Everett Dirksen was in and out. Agnew kept his own tally sheet. Two days before the vote was cast, he accurately predicted the outcome.

It was not uncommon to see him on the floor of the Senate, chatting quietly with its members, doing his homework. Agnew's political career had not included legislative experience. He was trying to make up for that lack. Few Vice-Presidents had ever appeared on the floor unless some earth-shaking vote was in prospect. Senators liked to have Agnew around.

But Nixon had put Agnew in charge of the Republician campaign to take over the Senate, and he was equal to the task. When Senator Edmund Muskie (D.-Me.), his Democratic opposite in the last Presidential campaign, proposed that the United States unilaterally halt weapons testing, it was Agnew who roared back that Muskie was "playing Russian roulette with U.S. security."

He zeroed in on Senator Vance Hartke (D.-Ind.) whom he accused of being "self-serving" and helping turn a proposed tax-reform measure into a "Rube Goldberg toy to entertain and attract reluctant voters to fading politicians." He called Senate Democrats "careless men . . . children playing with power tools."

They were stung to the quick, but their answers were no match for his sharp jabs. Of Senator William Proxmire's attacks on defense spending, he cracked: "We're getting a little worried about him. We think he's suffering from a military-industrial complex."

But it was with Senator Albert Gore, of Tennessee, uncle of the woman who had introduced him to Nixon, that he had his loudest wrangle.

It started innocently enough. After Agnew had denounced "effete snobs" and Moratorium leaders, reporters stopped Gore in the Senate hallway and asked his reaction.

"Vice-President Agnew," the Tennessee populist said, "is the greatest disaster this country has suffered since Vietnam."

Agnew was then interviewed by Frank Vanderlinden of the *Nashville Banner* and said that Senator Gore "has been inflicted" on the poeple of Tennessee long enough, it was time to defeat him and elect a Republican. He continued the attack on Gore in a speech to a Republican rally in New Orleans, and to the American Farm Bureau Federation in Washington. Gore had proposed a $1,000 personal income tax exemption, which the administration opposed. "My only thought," he said, "is that Senator Gore is living up to his name."

Gore came back with a sarcastic speech on the Senate floor. "The Vice-President is too modest," he said, tongue-in-cheek. "I am practically certain he has had other thoughts. And to adapt a phrase made famous by another distinguished statesman—if you gave me a week, I might be able to think of one."

Agnew was enjoying every minute of it. And he intended to step up the tempo.

IX

AGNEW VERSUS THE MEDIA

"The reason I spoke out was because . . . I had had enough."—Vice-President Spiro T. Agnew, in *Life,* November 28, 1969.

Agnew's ringing indictment of "effete snobs" who pass themselves off as intellectuals, his barefisted challenge to "those who prefer to side with the enemy rather than stand by this free nation" brought his own enemies out into the streets in a murderous mood. It was fair to chant, "Hey, hey, LBJ, how many kids did you kill today?", to refer sneeringly to "Tricky Dick," and to make crude jokes about the Vice-President. For Agnew to tear into the long-haired and the unwashed somehow betrayed his "lack of mental and moral sensitivity."

But they watched and listened. In the salons and embassies in Washington, cocktails grew watery and the canapés grew cold when Agnew came on the tube. Society writers chronicled that Senator Edward Kennedy, at a party in Washington—he was somewhere at a party every night—paled when the Vice-President paid his compliments to Averill Harriman. Harriman enjoyed the status of godhood in Kennedy circles, and the Senator stood murmuring, "appalling . . . unbelievable . . . I've got to do something." Anything Ted Kennedy could do in competition with Spiro Agnew, at that moment, wasn't a great deal.

Agnew was amused. He was enjoying himself.

"A little over a week ago," he told a Republican dinner in Harrisburg, Pennsylvania, on October 30, 1969, "I took a rather unusual step for a Vice-President. I said something."

He grinned and remarked: "It seems that by slaughtering a sacred cow, I triggered a holy war. I have no regrets. I do not intend to repudiate my beliefs, recant my words, or run and hide."

This was not according to the script. Agnew, challenged,

was expected to backtrack, to say he had been misunderstood, to try to make peace with the beautiful people.

He continued to speak, words and phrases the silent majority—Mr. and Mrs. Suburbaman—took as their own because he said what they believed. "Will citizens refuse to be led by a series of Judas goats down tortuous paths of illusion and self-destruction?" . . . "I believe in constitutional dissent. . . . I do not believe that demonstrations, lawful or unlawful, merit my approval or even my silence," . . . "I, for one, will not lower my voice until the restoration of sanity, and civil order, allows a quiet voice to be heard once again," . . . "Frightening forces have been set in motion as the public has become conditioned to precipitate action rather than quiet discussion," . . . "America today is drifting toward Plato's classic definition of a degenerating society . . . a democracy that permits the voice of the mob to dominate the affairs of government."

This, of course, betrayed the Vice-President's "lack of mental and moral sensitivity."

He said more: "In a modern society, the radical himself is in danger of becoming irrelevant . . . radical movements cannot survive in a democracy without violence." . . . "I am not ready to run up a white flag for the United States of America, and I don't think you are, either." . . . "These arrogant ones and their admirers in Congress who reach almost for equal arrogance at times, are asking us to repudiate principles that have made this country great. . . . They have a masochistic compulsion to destroy their country's strength." . . . "The American people appreciate the truth, and would rather have it than optimistic drivel . . . I do not overstate the case. If I am aware of the danger, the convicted rapist, Eldridge Cleaver, is aware of the potential."

He had chosen as his subject "Impudence in the Streets."

It was a revealing speech that clearly showed the beliefs of the man who, in a moment of tragedy, could become President of the United States.

Ten days earlier, on October 20, he had spoken at Jackson, Mississippi. The speech was widely interpreted and reported as a retreat in the government's demands for desegregation of Mississippi school districts. This, in part, is what he said.

Let it be made very clear that this administration will never appeal to a racist philosophy. . . . However, a free government cannot impose rules of social acceptance upon its citizens. Just so I won't be misunderstood by the pundits who read so many things into my speeches, I don't say I mean social acceptance between members of the same race or religion or between races and religions. The point is this—in a man's private life he has the right to make his own friends. Unfortunately, the legitimate cause of civil rights, a cause that I've fought hard for in my state both as a county official and as governor, has been all too frequently diverted, and even perverted in this direction. . . .

For too long the South has been the punching bag for those who characterize themselves as liberal intellectuals. Actually, they are constantly demonstrating the antithesis of intelligence. Their reactions are visceral, not intellectual, and they seem to believe that truth is revealed rather than systematically proved. . . . Their course is one of applause for our enemies and condemnation of our leaders. Their course is a course that will ultimately weaken and erode the very fiber of America . . . they arouse themselves into a continual emotional crescendo, substituting disruptive demonstrations for reason and precipitate action for persuasion.

. . . this is the group that believes in marching down the streets of America to protest the war in Vietnam to our President. They would never think of protesting the continuation of this war to the government that is actually continuing it—the government in Hanoi.

Finally, these leaders of the New Left would have America abdicate its position of leadership throughout the world. The fact that this position of leadership was conferred—in trust and respect—by the smaller and less powerful nations does not bother these men one whit. They would have us renounce our commitments and repudiate the 400,000 American lives sacrificed to the cause of world peace in this century. They would have America turn inward and vegetate in splendid isolation.

On November 10, 1969, he spoke to the National Municipal League in Philadelphia, an organization founded by the late Supreme Court Justice Louis Brandeis. Once again, he defended his country's values and struck out at the militants.

We forget that this nation was conceived and has continued

as an asylum for the world's oppressed. We overlook the fact today that our country remains the first choice among the world's immigrants.

Although we cannot be complacent about our faults, neither should we be apologetic about our strengths. Yet apology seems to be becoming our national posture. We have seen attempts to pervert the liberal virtue of self-criticism to the national vice of self-contempt.

. . . while there is a lot wrong with America, there is a lot more right with America. Our strengths outweigh our problems. Our potential is vast, and the time we waste on negative introspection could be far better invested in positive action.

Just because America has not implemented all the ideals of the Declaration of Independence and the Constitution does not mean that we should stop trying. Our inadequacies should be a spur to our improvement. If ever American society totally achieves its ideals, it will do so because those ideals have become unchallenging and ludicrously low . . .

. . . today's dissidents misdirect their fire when they attack the system. They should, instead, use the system to reform the institutions and establishments. . . . The Mob, the Mobilization, the Moratorium have become somewhat fashionable forms of citizen expression. But each suffers from the same flaws. . . . They are negative in content, disruptive in effect. They inflame emotions rather than stimulate solutions. Protest is every citizen's right, but that does not ensure that every protest is right. It simply protects every citizen's lawful protest, be it right or wrong.

[Ultimately, Agnew predicted] the popularity of mass street demonstrations will wane, just as we saw mass violence wane over the past year. And for the same reason: It is pointless. Turning out a few hundred thousand people in a nation of two hundred million proves nothing in the way of a public mandate. We can speed the demise of carnival in the streets by withholding our sympathy. We can blunt its adverse impact by seizing the initiative.

The body politic of America is not able to survive on adrenaline any better than on apathy. We are a mature nation, which means that we should be able to navigate a moderate course without being trapped on the shoals of mediocrity.

. . . Because intolerant clamor and cacophony rage about us, let us not be afraid to raise our voices in spirited defense of the best society the world has ever known. It is an alarm we sound—an alarm that must be audible to be heard. I, for one, will not lower my voice until the restoration of sanity and civil order allow a quiet voice to be heard once again.

But it was in Des Moines, Iowa, on November 13, that Agnew came into his own, and started a controversy that was not abated. In an address before the Midwest Regional Republican Committee, he took on the television networks.

A week earlier, President Nixon had gone on the tube to discuss Vietnam. Agnew said the President's intention was to "rally the American people to see the conflict through to a lasting and just peace." Nixon spoke for thirty-two minutes.

Almost immediately, the Vice-President declared, "his words and policies were subjected to instant analysis and querulous criticism." His audience of 70 million Americans was "inherited by a small band of network commentators and self-appointed analysts, the majority of whom expressed, in one way or another, their hostility to what he had to say. . . . It was obvious their minds were made up in advance."

One analyst, Agnew said, "twice contradicted the President's statement about the exchange of correspondence with Ho Chi Minh." Another challenged his ability as a politician. Another said he was "following the Pentagon line." By their expression on their faces, the tones of their questions, and the sarcasm of their response, they made clear their sharp disapproval.

The audience loved what Agnew said. So did a vast television audience, not, however, including Ted Kennedy or anyone in the front offices of ABC, CBS, or NBC.

One network, Agnew said, "trotted out Averill Harriman for the occasion. Throughout the President's address, he waited in the wings. When the President concluded, Mr. Harriman recited perfectly. He attacked the Thieu government [in Saigon] as unrepresentative; he criticized the President's speech for its various deficiencies; he twice issued a call to the Senate Foreign Relations Committee to debate Vietnam once again; he [said] the Viet Cong and the North Vietnamese did not really want a military takeover in South Vietnam; he told a little anecdote about a very, very responsible fellow he had met in the North Vietnamese delegation."

Agnew was not through with Harriman.

"A word about Mr. Harriman," he continued. "For ten months he was America's chief negotiatior at the Paris peace talks—a period in which the United States swapped some of the greatest military concessions in the history of warfare for an enemy agreement in the shape of a bargaining table. Like Coleridge's Ancient Mariner, Mr. Harriman seems to be under some heavy compulsion to justify his failures to anyone who will listen. The networks have shown themselves willing to give him all the air time he deserves."

Agnew paid tribute to television where it was due. He said they had made hunger and black lung national issues overnight. They had done "what no other medium" could have done in dramatizing the horrors of war. They "have tackled our most difficult social problems with a directness and immediacy that is the gift of their medium." They have "focused the nation's attention on its environmental abuses, on pollution in the Great Lakes and the threatened ecology of the Everglades."

But he also charged that television "elevated Stokely Carmichael and George Lincoln Rockwell [late head of the American Nazi Party] from obscurity into national prominence . . . a raised eyebrow, an inflection of the voice, a caustic remark dropped in the middle of a broadcast can raise doubts in a million minds about the veracity of a public official or the wisdom of a government policy."

The men who set these policies, he said, are a "small group . . . numbering no more than a dozen anchormen, commentators, and executive producers."

And, he went on, "to a man" these commentators and producers live and work in the geographical and intellectual confines of Washington, D.C. and New York City, the latter of which James Reston [of *The New York Times*] terms 'the most unrepresentative community in the entire United States.' Both communities bask in their own provincialism, their own parochialism . . . these men read the same newspapers and draw their political and social views from the same sources. Worse, they talk constantly to one another, thereby providing artificial reinforcement for their shared views."

Agnew denied the network claims they were entitled to the same first amendment protection as newspapers. "The situations are not identical," he insisted. "Where *The New York Times* reaches 800,000 people. NBC reaches twenty-five times that number with its evening news. Nor can the tremendous impact of seeing television film and hearing commentary be compared with the reading of the printed page."

He quoted Walter Lippmann in saying that "the networks, which are few in number, have a virtual monopoly of a whole medium of communication."

"A virtual monopoly of a whole medium of communication is something a democratic people can blithely ignore," Agnew concluded.

In television, he went on, "Gresham's law seems to be operating. Bad news drives out good news. The irrational is more controversial than the rational. Concurrence can no longer compete with dissent. One minute of Eldridge Cleaver is worth ten minutes of Roy Wilkins. The labor crisis settled at the negotiationg table is nothing compared to the confrontation that results in a strike—or better yet, violence along the picket line. Normality has become the nemesis of the evening news.

"The upshot is . . . that a narrow and distorted picture of America often emerges from the television news. A single, dramatic piece of the mosiac becomes, in the minds of millions, the whole picture. The American who relies upon television for his news might conclude that the majority of American students are embittered radicals; that the majority of black Americans feel no regard for their country; that violence and lawlessness are the rule, rather than the exception, on American campuses. None of these conclusions is true."

Agnew suggested that "the place to start looking for a credibility gap is not in government in Washington but in the studios of the networks in New York."

There have seldom been scenes like the ones that followed. Not only had Agnew attacked television as a medium— permissible, within limits—he had directly challenged its commentators. These men were not accustomed to that. Like Agnew, they had risen to the status of folk heroes. Most of them drew salaries which ran into six figures, many were millionaires, some got up to $5,000 for a public appearance. The Vice-President was striking directly at their pocketbooks.

The network presidents defended their organizations. Julian Goodman, president of NBC, said Agnew "evidently would prefer a different kind of television reporting, one that would be subservient to whatever political group was in authority."

ABC's Leonard Goldstein said: "We will continue to report the news accurately and fully, confident in the ultimate judgment of the American public."

CBS president Frank Stanton said Agnew's speech was "an unprecedented attempt to intimidate a news medium."

Most newscasters reported the Des Moines speech as straight news, with some emphasis on their boss's reply. David Brinkley of NBC was a bit more argumentative; he wasn't "going to get down in the gutter with this guy." Walter Cronkite was puzzled; what could Agnew be talking about?

By all odds the strongest reply came from CBS and Dr. Stanton. As time went by, CBS and its president seemed unwilling to drop the matter.

Stanton chose as his forum 750 members of the International Radio and Television Society, an organization of industry executives, at New York's Plaza Hotel. The speech was broadcast live over CBS Radio, and later sent out on video tape to its television stations, so important did Dr. Stanton rate his reply.

Agnew, he said, "does not seem to have been walking a lonely path in the direction of supression and harassment. In my judgment, the whole tone, the whole content, and the whole pattern of this government intrusion into the substance and methods of the broadcast press, and indeed all of journalism, have the gravest implication.

"In the context of this intimidation, the self-serving disavowal of no censorship, no matter how often repeated, is meaningless."

Agnew's attack "is ominous," Stanton said, because it was made "upon the journalism of a medium licensed by the government of which he is a high-ranking officer."

Stranton's protest became so strong that the *Washington Post*—which later came under Agnew's attack—editorially told him to pipe down, it wasn't all that big a threat to press freedom.

Agnew, surprisingly, got support from the American Civil Liberties Union. "Some things are true even if Vice-Presidents say them," remarked John deJ. Pemberton, Jr., ACLU executive secretary.

And Lee Huebner, a former president of the liberal Ripon Society and now a White House assistant, said that television executives were "overreacting." Huebner told the Speech

Association of America, meeting in Washington, that Mr. Agnew was merely "trying to wake up" people.

"Walter Cronkite, CBS's show horse, was almost as perturbed as Frank Stanton. Cronkite chose as his forum a civic club luncheon in St. Joseph, Missouri, his hometown. St. Joseph is inordinately proud of Cronkite; it could be counted on to deal gently with him in the question-and-answer period, even if most of its Middle American types secretly agreed with Agnew.

Walter Cronkite was all injured pride and innocence. Didn't the Vice-President know that Cronkite had been born in Missouri, Eric Severeid in South Dakota, Dan Rather in Georgia, David Brinkley in North Carolina, Frank McGee in Oklahoma? Cronkite seemed to be saying, "Look, we're all a bunch of country boys."

Richard Nixon had been pilloried during the Eisenhower-Stevenson campaign when he was called on to defend his secret campaign fund. His "Checkers" speech drew the scorn of the nation's media.

By comparison, St. Joe made Checkers look good.

The response was overwhelming. Even Agnew had not accurately gauged—perhaps even the American people did not know—how deeply, how personally, millions of Americans resented the TV anchormen who nightly professed to tell them what they should believe, trampled on their traditional values and seemed to scorn the things they so deeply believed. The telegrams and phone calls poured in. This writer has personal knowledge of the havoc this outpouring of support for the Vice-President caused in Washington. I had delivered a speech on Vietnam that evening in Pulaski, Virginia, and found myself snowed in at Roanoke.

Assistant Secretary of the Navy Don Hittle, a retired Marine brigadier general, was hosting a lunch at noon the next day for retired Air Force Lieutenant General Emmett J. "Rosie" O'Donnell, president of the USO. From Roanoke I sent a telegram explaining my predicament and expressing my regrets I could not attend. When I arrived home twenty-four hours later, I found it had not yet been delivered. In a rage, I called the Western Union manager.

He said the response to Agnew's speech had been so great that "we still have telegrams all over the floor; some have been there since last night."

Even more interesting was the reaction of the commentators the next time the President spoke to the nation. These were not, it turned out, brave men, battlers who, like Spiro Agnew, had no intention of recanting.

They had already caved in. This time there was no Averill Harrimans, or Frank Mankewitzs, or Tom Bradens, to define the world and its people in the peculiar terms they see it. There was not even the usual covey of commentators sitting around smiling at one another while they prepared to deliver Delphic pronouncements. ABC had two men; CBS three, NBC no more. They had no personal views to pass on. They told their audience simply, directly, what the President had said, and signed off. That of course we already knew. They seemed terribly glad to escape.

Nor have they regained their courage since. Two and one-half months later, on January 22, 1970, when President Nixon delivered his State of the Union Message to Congress, the big question was what the commentators would say afterward.

NBC and CBS confined themselves to brief fifteen-minute summaries, noticably devoid of criticism. When CBS's Roger Mudd forget himself enough to ask Dan Rather what he thought the President's motives might be, Rather said only that it is "very difficult to read anyone's motives." But the President's objectives were clear, he added.

Eric Severeid praised the President for "pathbreaking" and seemed only mildly curious why he hadn't said more about the war and about racial conflict.

ABC abandoned its studio format and went looking for guest experts around the country. They interviewed an Omaha banker; a former mayor of Detroit; Charles Evers, black mayor of Fayette, Mississippi; and former Governor George Wallace of Alabama. Most of these mentioned the things President Nixon did not talk about. Former Mayor Jerome Cavanaugh of Detroit wondered why he hadn't attacked the problems of the cities more vigorously, Evers was concerned with the problems of black people, and Wallace said he should have talked about what integration is doing to the school system. ABC also produced a panel which included Senator Muskie, Senator Gaylord Nelson (D.-Wis.) and Senator Howard Baker (R.-Tenn.). Not a Harriman in the bunch.

"There is no doubt," columnist Robert Novak said later on

another TV show, "that Mr. Agnew did scare the dickens out of the people in TV."

The anguished screams continued from television, from Congress, and from the press.

Hubert Humphrey had to get into the act of course. Having been skewered by television at the Democratic Convention in Chicago—treatment from which he never did completely recover—he was still ready to defend those who had questioned his courage a year earlier—if, in doing so, he could get in a poke at the Republicans. The former Vice-President charged the Nixon administration with a "calculated attack" on the right of dissent and on the television media.

Mr. Agnew was amused. "Let us leave Mr. Humphrey to his own conscience," he said. "America already has too many politicians who would rather switch than fight."

A member of Congress charged Agnew with "a creeping socialistic scheme against the free enterprise broadcast industry." A television critic said his Des Moines speech was "disgraceful, ignorant, and base," that it would lead us as a nation "into an ugly era of the most fearsome suppression and intimidation." Still another found it "one of the most sinister speeches I have ever heard made by a public official." He was charged with an "appeal to prejudice."

"And they say I have a thin skin," Agnew said.

He said his critics "do not address themselves to the questions I have raised. In fairness, others—a majority of the critics and commentators—did take up the main thrust of my address. And if the debate they have engaged in continues, our goal will surely be reached: a thorough self-examination by the networks of their own policies, and, perhaps, prejudices. That was my objective then; it is my objective now."

Agnew was amused, but there were times, he said, when the criticism hurt. "It is not an easy thing to wake up each morning to learn that some prominent man or institution has implied that you are a bigot, a racist, or a fool," he said.

His old friends on *The New York Times* had taken him to task over his Jackson, Mississippi, speech in which he raked student militants over the coals. "He [Agnew] lambasted the nation's youth in sweeping and ignorant generalizations, when it is clear to all perceptive observers that American youth today is far more imbued with idealism, a sense of service, and a deep humanitarianism that any generation in recent history, including particularly Mr. Agnew's," *The Times* said.

Agnew shot back that that was a

> slur on a generation that brought America out of the Great Depression without resorting to the extremes of either facism or Communism. . . . it is a strange thing to say about an entire generation that helped to provide greater material blessings and personal freedom—out of that Depression—for more people than any other nation in history.

> Just as millions of young Americans in this generation have shown valor and courage and heroism in fighting the longest and least popular war in our history, so it was that the young men of my generation went ashore at Normandy under Eisenhower and with MacArthur into the Philippines.

> . . . Whatever freedom exists today in Western Europe and Japan exists because hundreds of thousands of young men in my generation are lying in graves in North Africa and France and Korea and a score of islands in the Western Pacific.

> This might not be considered enough of a "sense of service" or "deep humanitarianism" for the "perceptive critics" who write editorials for *The New York Times,* but it's good enough for me, and I am content to let history be the judge.

Agnew said he knew, of course, how to get along with the media. He spelled it out in his article in *Life* on November 28.

> It does not take great perception to know that if an elected official advocates certain policies and eschews others, he will not only get good news space but editorial plaudits. If all an elected official wants is a good press, he has only to recite certain accepted precepts . . . and most of the media will respond with a conditioned accolade to the ringing phrase. Couching it in negative terms, if an elected official wants to avoid a bad press, all he has to do is fuzz the controversial issues or carefully work his way around them.

> But what kind of leader is this? More importantly, what sort of human being is this? Someone who values expediency at best, would not be above deceit at worst . . .

Now he was ready to take on the press—certainly its most powerful bastions—something no other politician has dared in recent times. The resentments that had built up since the early days of his governorship in Annapolis overflowed in a torrent of angry words. They came at Montgomery, Alabama, on November 29—one week after his Des Moines speech—in an address to the chamber of commerce.

He chose as his targets the *Washington Post* and *The New York Times,* an organization the late Westbrook Pegler had said "maintains its own consular service," so complete is its global coverage.

He charged that the *Post,* owned by Katherine Graham, not only controls the largest newspaper in the nation's capital and also owns *Newsweek* magazine, one of Washington's four television stations, and an all-news radio station, "all grinding out the same editorial line."

"This is not a subject you have seen debated on the editorial pages of the *Washington Post* or *The New York Times,*" he said. "For the purpose of clarity, before my thoughts are obliterated in the smoking typewriters of my friends in Washington and New York, let me emphasize I am not recommending the dismemberment of the Washington Post Company. I am merely pointing out that the public should be aware that these four powerful voices hearken to the same master."

He charged that when some 300 congressmen and fifty-nine senators signed a letter endorsing the President's policies in Vietnam, it was big news even in the *Post* and the *Baltimore Sun,* "scarcely house organs for the Nixon administration." Yet *The New York Times* "did not carry a word." He said that Pope Paul had applauded the President's efforts to end the war in Vietnam, and endorsed the way he was proceeding. *The Times* played the story on page 11.

"The day when the network commentators and even gentlemen of *The New York Times* enjoyed a form of diplomatic immunity from comment and criticism of what they have said—that day is over," Agnew declared.

They loved it in Montgomery. And they loved it all over the country. Most newspapermen—including this one—have had but a hazy idea of how deeply we are distrusted by those who read us. Part of this of couse is attributable to the fact that we are constantly bringing bad news. In other days, James Reston once said, they used to hang the courier who brought bad tidings; now they give him a Pulitzer Prize. But part of it is attributable to the fact that, on the Eastern

Seaboard particularly, many top writers have become intellectual snobs, looking down on, when they are not lecturing, their readers. They are alienated from the majority of their fellow citizens.

Arthur Ochs Sulzberger, president and publisher of *The New York Times*, said Agnew was "in error when he implies that *The New York Times* ever sought or enjoyed immunity from criticism . . . all American institutions from the press to the Presidency should be subject of free and open debate."

He said the Vice-President was mistaken when he said *The Times* did not carry a word about the congressmen and senators who had endorsed the President's Vietnam policy.

"Unfortunately," he added, "it failed to make the edition that reached Washington but was carried in a later edition of *The Times*."

He said *The Times* had "given considerable attention to that story as it developed." The story about Pope Paul, he said, was on page 3, not page 11.

"The Vice-President unfortunately does not understand some of the complicated problems of making up a newspaper," Mr. Sulzberger said. "Many important stories have to appear on pages other than page 1."

Mrs. Graham said the *Post* and other members of its corporate family "decidedly do not grind out the same editorial line. It is a long-standing policy of the Post company to enlist in each of its enterprises the best professional journalists we can find and give them a maximum of freedom in which to work. They disagree on many issues."

What Agnew said about the *Post* and *The Times* took but a few paragraphs of his Montgomery speech. Naturally it drew the most attention. The bulk of his address—although it was headed "The Power of the Press"—once again was devoted to young America, particularly the dissidents.

I have not and do not condemn this generation of young Americans [Agnew declared]. Like Edmund Burke, I would not know how to "draw up an indictment against a whole people." They are our sons and daughters. They contain in their number many gifted, idealistic, and courageous young men and women.

But they also enlist in their number an arrogant few who march under the flags and portraits of dictators, who intimi-

date and harass university professors, who use gutter obsceni-
ties to shout down speakers with whom they disagree, who
openly profess their belief in the efficacy of violence in a
democratic society.

My generation had its own breed of losers, and our generation dealt with them through the courts, our laws, and our
system. The challenge now is for the new generation to put
its own house in order.

He quoted Dr. Sidney Hook ("storm troopers"), Arnold
Beichman ("young Jacobins"), Walter Lacquer ("cultural
and political idiocies"), and Irving Kristol ("Radical students
find it possible to be genuinely heartsick at the injustices and
brutalities of American society, while approving of injustice
and brutality in the name of the revolution.").

"These are not names drawn at random from the letter-
head of an Agnew-for-Vice-President committee," Agnew
said. "These are men more eloquent and erudite than I."

He predicted that soon voices will be raised in Congress to
permit the return of young men who have fled to Canada and
Sweden to avoid military service, that they will be called
"young and misguided American boys" and "from a small
minority they will get a heroes' welcome."

"They are not our heroes," he said flatly. "Many of our
heroes will not be coming home; some are coming back in
hospital ships, without limbs or eyes, with scars they shall
carry the rest of their lives.

"Should I remain silent while what these heroes have done
is villified by some as a 'dirty and immoral' war and criticized
by others as no more than a war brought on by the chauvin-
istic anti-Communism of Presidents Kennedy, Johnson, and
Nixon?"

Agnew said his critics say he is polarizing the nation. He
charged that those who marched in the October Moratorium
"sought to polarize the American people against the President's policy in Vietnam.

"That is their right," he said, "and so it is my right and
duty to stand up and speak out for the value in which I believe. How can you ask the man in the street in this country
to stand up for what he believes if his own elected leaders
weasel and cringe? . . . my political and journalistic adver-
saries sometimes seem to be asking that I circumscribe my
rhetorical freedom, while they place no restriction on theirs."

The *Post* and *The Times* may not have liked the way Agnew talked, but others did. Editorialized the Gowrie, Iowa (population 1,103) *Times*:

> Vice-President Agnew's outspokenness with respect to the militant Left, peace marchers, and alleged one-sided press and TV coverage of President Nixon's views on Vietnam have struck many as welcome confirmation of their own feelings and opinions.
>
> . . . After Agnew had stepped on some editorial toes it wasn't too surprising then that the oversensitive national press has continued to make him a target for their not too subtle abuse and aren't about to let up on him for a while, at least.
>
> It has been daily downgrading his visit to Asia, questioning the value of such a trip and quickly jumping on any miscues in speech or action. . . . As far as we are concerned, Vice-President Agnew has put his foot in his mouth on occasion, but at least he's no fence-straddler and isn't afraid to speak out on the issues.
>
> Like the outspoken Harry "Give 'em Hell" Truman, Agnew is proving that the right to genuine dissent is still very much alive in the best American tradition. And despite the hue and cry of the nation's TV editors, there's very little likelihood that there will be anything bordering on censorship arising as a result.

What he said in Des Moines and Montgomery and Harrisburg and Philadelphia and Jackson, he said later in Washington and Baltimore and Hot Springs, Arkansas. To many Americans he had become a prophet around whom they could rally.

This, in retrospect, was the man from Annapolis they said "abhorred speechmaking," but who now found his speeches preserved, quoted, and reprinted by the hundreds of thousands. There were those who hated him, who shrank from the lash of his tongue. But he would not be silent. He was not afraid. He had committed political suicide at Baltimore on April 11, 1968, and miraculously survived.

He was still on his way.

X

AGNEW TODAY—A POTPOURRI

It had been one of those story-book romances.

Soon after President Nixon had named his Cabinet, he gave a White House reception for Cabinet members and thier families.

Many were strangers to each other.

Douglas Rogers, son of the new Secretary of State, was there and so was Nancy Hardin, daughter of the Chancellor of Nebraska University, who had been appointed Secretary of Agriculture.

It was love at first sight.

Douglas' mother recalls that as soon as he spotted Nancy he whispered: "Let's get better acquainted with the Hardins."

Their engagement was announced a few months later, and on January 31, 1970, they were married in Washington with President Nixon attending.

The night before, Attorney General John N. Mitchell and his peripatetic wife Martha gave a cocktail-buffet for the young couple. The Mitchells' Watergate apartment was loaded with big names, good food, and sparkling conversation.

But it was the Vice-President of the United States, Spiro T. Agnew, who made it the success it was. The highlight of the evening came when he played a romantic piece for the young people on the Mitchells' grand piano while Nancy and Doug looked over his shoulder. He even offered to play a duet with Martha Mitchell on her Hammond organ but, uncharacteristically, she demurred.

At fifty-one, as he begins his second year as Vice-President, Agnew is the first to admit he has had a great— "an unbelievable"—year. He attributes this to President Nixon's faith in making him a full member of the White House team. His health is good; his personal physician, Dr. Emmett Queen, chief of medical education at Baltimore's Bon Secour Hospital, says he has never known a man to be in better health. His weight is down from 195 when he was nominated to a sleek 180. He intends to keep it there, not only because he feels better, but because self-discipline, he says, is good for a man. He eschews the elevators in the Executive Office-Building, across barricaded Executive Avenue from the White House, and sprints up its winding staircase. Staff members and others who feel compelled to sprint with him sometimes arrive winded on the third or fourth floor. The Vice-President isn't even breathing heavily.

As the nation's second couple, the Agnews necessarily are part of the Washington social scene. They are out several nights a week; during a recent week, the Vice-President and Mrs. Agnew were away from home six out of seven evenings. Too often this means getting home before eight P.M., changing to white tie or tux, and "making an appearance" for an hour or so at some occasion someone feels he shouldn't miss. Just enough, he grumbles, to ruin my evening and make it impossible to do any of the things you'd like.

Once they arrive, their natural conviviality usually takes over the and the Agnews enjoy themselves. Washingtonians who follow the society pages have grown used to reading news such as that the queen of the Capital's Mardi Gras Ball, Emily Elizabeth Tucker Peevey of Memphis, entered the Shoreham Hotel ballroom "on the arm of Vice-President Spiro Agnew and made a grand sweep of the room, anointing more than 1,500 people with queenly spirit before ascending to the throne. . . ."

The Agnews sat at the table of Senator and Mrs. Russell Long of Louisiana but "departed before the dancing."

But the Agnews' roots and hearts are still in Maryland. Washington's big-time hostesses—who made an industry out of entertaining—have been unable, so far, to capture Ted and Judy and add them to their menages. Not that they haven't tried.

Maryland, of course, is next door to Washinpton, D.C. Two of its largest counties—Montgomery and Prince Georges—are Washington bedrooms. Baltimore and Annapolis each are thirty miles away. Towson is an hour-and-a-half's drive. Agnew is easily accessible to men like George White, Sam Kimmel, and Judge Barrett. He will see them even if someone of national stature must wait.

Other Vice-Presidents have come from more distant places

—Texas, Kentucky, Missouri, California, Iowa, Kansas. It has not been as easy for them to keep in touch with home folks. Gradually they have become authentic Washingtonians. So far, that has not happened to the Agnews.

Agnew clings stubbornly to his old friends. When he arrived back from his Far Eastern trip, his first speech was to 900 Marylanders at an inn outside Baltimore. Ths opposition of newspapers elsewhere he can take in stride; there is real bitterness in his feeling for the Baltimore papers, which have fought him since his April 11, 1968, speech to Negro leaders. Most people in Maryland read nothing but the *Sun*; that it should be down on him is, as far as Agnew is concerned, hard to forgive.

When the Baltimore County Bar Association held its annual get-together in February, 1970, Spiro T. Agnew—member—was there. His successor as governor, Marvin Mandel, was the principal speaker and Agnew did not begrudge him the podium. He was content to sit in the audience.

When President Nixon delivered his State of the Union Message to the Congress, Agnew and venerable John McCormack (D.-Mass.), speaker of the House of Representatives, presided. But later the Agnews took lunch in the Members Dining Room with a couple whom Washington society reporters kissed off as a "Maryland doctor and his wife."

Dr. Emmett Queen is Agnew's closest friend. It is a personal, not a political relationship. The two became friends when they were teen-agers. Agnew went to Forest Park High School and Queen to Loyola. Queen's sister and Judy Judefield—who was to become Mrs. Agnew—were close friends, too.

In their teens, the two boys borrowed the Queen family car and drove to Canada for ten days. "Come to think of it," Dr. Queen says now, "I don't think Spiro was old enough to drive. I was sixteen or seventeen and he was a year and one-half younger." Hugh and Henry Power, sons of the Episcopal minister who had baptized Agnew, went along. Hugh Power is now a physician in Texas and Henry is an Episcopal minister in New Jersey.

One summer, Queen recalls, the four saved their money from odd jobs to buy a pool table for the church basement.

Queen is the Agnew family physician. He attended both of Agnew's parents until they died.

Agnew took Queen in his campaign party as his official physician. The doctor protested that he had "never had anything to do with politics." Agnew opined there wasn't anything very political about a bad cold or a broken arm; he knew medicine, didn't he? Dr. Queen took a two-months leave from Bon Secour Hospital. He says now it was just for the ride; he had very little to do.

Like Mrs. Agnew, Dr. Queen calls the Vice-President by his proper name, Spiro. Others, who would like to know him better, usually call him Ted.

Agnew has maintained other contacts in his home country. He is particularly loyal to those who were his friends when he was a struggling young lawyer. If he needs a haircut, for instance, he is likely to call for his old friend Ken Smith to drive over to Washington. If he can spare the time, he will drive over to Baltimore to Charles Armetta's Hair Styling Shop—that's what it's called now—in the Tower Building, where Smith has a chair. Dr. Queen remembers running into Smith once at Government House in Annapolis. After he had finished cutting Agnew's hair, the three enjoyed a game of pool in the governatorial recreation room.

They knew each other as youngsters, and the friendship has continued. Armetta tells of Agnew's dropping by his shop when he was Vice-President-elect. Armetta was out. The Vice-President-to-be wrote in Armetta's appointment book: "Charlie, don't you ever work?" and sat down to wait.

He is also close to Joe Canzanni and Sabatino Luperini, who operate Sabatino's Restaurant. He sometimes drops in unannounced, as he did when he was studying law and could barely afford the price of a meal. Now, however, he is accompanied by Secret Service agents. Four stay downstairs, four go upstairs with the Vice-President. Sabatino's is the kind of restaurant that has red-and-white-checkered tablecloths. Agnew never reserves a table; he takes whatever is available. His favorite dish is linguini with white clam sauce and a salad. His old friends won't let him pay now, but he is a generous tipper.

Ken Smith, the barber, was a guest on Air Force Two, which flew to Cape Kennedy for the Apollo 11 moonshot.

A typical Agnew day—if there is one—begins around nine A.M. when he arrives in his chauffeured limousine from his Shoreham Hotel apartment. Once a week, there is a congressional leadership breakfast at the White House with men like

Representative Jerry Ford (R.-Mich.), the House minority leader; Representative Leslie Arends (R.-Ill.), the House GOP whip; Senator Hugh Scott (R.Pa.), the Senate's minority leader; and Senator Robert Griffin (R.-Mich.), the Senate Republican whip.

This means the Vice-President, never a particularly early riser, must be on hand before eight A.M.

During the remainder of his morning, there could be a Cabinet meeting—Agnew, unlike Dawes in the Coolidge administration, is very much a part of any Cabinet discussion—or one of the National Security Council on which he has a seat.

Invariably there is what C. Stanley Blair, his right-hand man, calls "some sort of council involvement." Agnew's leadership of Presidential commissions already makes a formidable list, and is growing.

He may meet with the Council on Space and Technology, the Council on Indian Affairs, the Council on Youth Opportunity, or the heads of the Office of Inter-Governmental Relations. His schedule is never the same from day to day.

The Vice-President has two offices. One is in the Executive Office Building, that gingerbready, otherworldly old monstrosity across from the White House. Originally it was the State-War-Navy Building when government was small enough to house three Cabinet departments in one building. Many say now that it is so ugly it is almost beautiful.

The other is in the Capitol, just off the Senate Chamber.

For several months after his inauguration he spent most of his time on Capitol Hill. He felt it was necessary to learn the Senate's customs and traditions, to get to know its members. He was frequently spotted from the press gallery. Since May, 1969, however, he has devoted more of his time to his downtown office.

If he plans to go to the Senate, if there is to be a close vote he may be called on to break, for instance, his driver is alerted that he'll be ready to leave around eleven A.M. Both Houses of Congress convene at noon. It's a fifteen-minute drive from the Executive Office Building to Capitol Hill.

The rest of his day is filled with political meetings, council agenda, and staff consultations. He usually leaves for home at 7:30, after the worst of Washington's evening rush hour is over.

The day after the Vice-President revealed on CBS's *Face*

the Nation on February 1, 1970, that President Nixon planned to set up a Cabinet-level committee to guide Southern school districts into court-ordered integration in "the least disruptive manner"—and that Agnew would head it—Agnew ran into Daniel Patrick Moynihan, Nixon's adviser on domestic affairs, in the Executive Dining Room at the White House.

Moynihan was one of those Agnew had told the nation would be a member, along with Attorney General Mitchell, HEW Secretary Robert Finch, and Presidential Assistant Bryce Harlow, who was eating at another table.

"It's not going to be a crowd-pleaser, Pat," he said. "I've had a dozen calls already this morning. No, I'm afraid it won't be a crowd-pleaser, at all."

Moynihan grinned ruefully.

An increasing number of the tasks Agnew has undertaken for his President in their first year in office could hardly be called crowd-pleasers. Some claim he has spoken for the President—has said things Nixon cannot say—as in his lashing of the media. He has had to take bad news to the nation's governors, disappoint the nation's mayors, confront the black militants, face angry American Indians, and explain failures not his own.

Yet, withal, the man has been a crowd-pleaser of the first magnitude. Polls now show him the third most popular man in the nation, behind President Nixon and evangelist Billy Graham. His name has become a household—in fact, an internationally recognizable—word.

It is, some say, part of the Agnew mystique.

Privately, the Vice-President says he "had no place to go but up."

"I don't think any Vice-Presidential candidate ever took the beating, the pounding, we did during that campaign," he says in bitter recollection. (Anyone who thinks Agnew is about to forgive and forget is mistaken; this man will endure many things, but he does not suffer insult lightly.) "It was constant and it was coordinated. We finally decided all we could do was ride it out. That wasn't easy."

His press secretary, Herb Thompson, nodded.

Agnew paused and went on: "Even at the Inauguration, many people felt the reason President Nixon won by so narrow a margin was because I pulled him down."

In the months intervening, something about this man has

caught the imagination of the American public. Whatever it is, it is uniquely his. He speaks for that entity now called the "silent majority" in a way few men before have spoken.

You get the feeling that Agnew himself does not always fully realize how far he has come.

"They could do it to me again," he remarked of his treatment during the 1968 campaign. He apparently is unaware that it is one thing to pillory an unknown, quite another to bring down a man who has attained his stature.

Cynthia Rosenwald is his attractive thirty-three-year-old speechwriter and research assistant. She is also mother and wife of a Baltimore Hecht Company (department stores) executive. She commutes between Washington and Baltimore three, sometimes four, days a week.

Half-jokingly, she likes to say her husband is the one person she knows who "hates" the Vice-President, her story that nothing Spiro Agnew could do could ever please Peter Rosenwald. Spiro Agnew's demands on Mrs. Rosenwald's time are too heavy, he says, they keep her away from her home and her family. Peter Rosenwald would like his wife to stop this nonsense and let him earn the family living.

Yet, she recalled recently, even Peter can be moved by Agnew. Watching him on TV not long ago, Rosenwald blurted to his wife: "My God, Cynnie, the man *has* got charisma!"

(Peter Rosenwald finally won out; Cynthia left the Vice President's staff in February. Herb Thompson said the parting was amicable, that she "simply wanted to spend more time with her family." Any work she does for Mr. Agnew now will be done at home in Baltimore.)

There can be little doubt that Agnew thoroughly enjoys his job. He likes to travel, and there is plenty of that, at home and abroad. He likes the association with people he used only to read about; he was Bob Hope's guest at Hope's posh golf tournament in California. He likes to be in the center of things, to feel that he is a shaker and a mover. He appreciates a good political scrap; Agnew is essentially a political animal. When Senator Charles Goodell (R.-N.Y.) unleashed a bitter attack on the Nixon Vietnamization program before the Senate Foreign Relations Committee, Agnew, in reply, managed somehow to concentrate his guns not on Republican Goodell but on "the opposition party." He enjoys the applause. He can even take satisfaction from the picketing and demonstrations that crop up wherever he goes ... "if a man didn't make *that* kind of enemy sometime in a political career, he wouldn't be worth much, would he?"

Does he work as hard as he did as governor of Maryland?

"I'm not underworked," he says slowly. "I don't have as many administrative decisions, the tough ones involving what to do about education, welfare, schools, the things that affect the daily lives of people. I have much more to do in a supportive role; that is one of my jobs, to back up the President. And the political demands are heavy."

The political demands in 1969 meant seventy-seven major speeches, some of which skyrocketed him into the national limelight and made him one of the most controversial—the most loved or most hated—Vice-Presidents of all time. There were a few hundred more appearances where he was expected to say a few words—which sometimes ran on into longish speeches.

These same demands also sent him on a series of fund-raising appearances around the country.

"The requests for him as a speaker, you wouldn't believe," Mrs. Rosenwald says. "It would be impossible—literally impossible—for him to fill even a small part of them. He's very much in demand."

Yet this is the same man, someone remarked, they once claimed "abhorred speechmaking."

"He's grown," Cynthia Rosenwald says. "In one year, you could almost feel him grow. He's more confident, more mature."

"There's been a tremendous growth factor here," Stanley Blair says. "This is a man who is still growing. The potential, the strength, the ability was always there. Now, it has been brought out."

It is doubtful that Spiro Agnew ever really abhorred speechmaking. He is a born wordsmith. He loves words, he plays on them like a violinist, and they come out well-shaped and rounded to say precisely what he means them to say. Words work for him; and he knows how to use them.

How does he build up a speech?

Mrs. Rosenwald's office is directly across the hall from his in the EOB. She is "always feeding him ideas," she keeps a file on all he has said, or might say, about any conceivable subject. In a sense, she knows how he thinks—and how he expresses himself—better than he does.

She insists, however, that she is not a speechwriter. She claims she is a researcher, that she fell into the job of speechwriting when a man selected for it washed out.

She first met the Vice-President at a reception in June, 1966, during the early stages of his campaign for the governorship. Cynthia was one semester short of her graduation from Goucher College, delayed by marriage and childbirth.

Mrs. Rosenwald recalls that she was having a drink later with Robert Goodman, head of a Baltimore public relations firm, Robert Goodman Associates. Goodman was "debating whether to take the Agnew or Finan account." (Attorney General Finan was seeking the Democratic nomination for governor.)

"Take Agnew," she suggested, "he's better-looking."

"That remark of mine will give you some idea of how politically savvy I am," Mrs. Rosenwald says now.

A week later Goodman called to say he had. He has since become adept at helping elect Republican governors in normally Democratic states. Among others, he's handled Republican Linwood Holton in Virginia, Arch More in West Virginia, and Louie Nunn in Kentucky.

Mrs. Rosenwald went to work for Agnew, through her connection with Goodman, and stayed on for a three-day-a-week stint when he became governor. With his election as Vice-President, it was only natural he transfer her to Washington. (Agnew also has his counterpart for Rose Mary Woods, Nixon's private secretary who has been with him for years. Alice Fringer, who sits in the Vice-President's outer office, started with Chris Kahl when he was Baltimore County executive, stayed on with Agnew, and now is in Washington.)

"Research assistant—which I am—is just an officeworker," Mrs. Rosenwald says firmly. "He writes his speeches. All I do is keep files."

Mrs. Rosenwald, it turns out, gets a weekly schedule of the Vice-President's public appearances at least two weeks in advance. If she doesn't, someone in his scheduling office hears about it. Then, she says, "I walk into his office and ask him, 'Well, sir, what would you like to tell such-and-such a group?' Sometimes the range is limited. You'd talk to cattlemen about cattle. But he might also want to say something about taxes. Or pollution."

If he wants to discuss a matter over which some particular department has jurisdiction, Mrs. Rosenwald files a priority request to be brought up-to-date on what they've done and plan to do.

She checks the Library of Congress.

Then she writes the first draft of his speech.

"That's when the fun begins," she says. "I'll go back in a little while and ask how he likes it. He'll say, invariably, it is the best I ever wrote. Then he begins rewriting it. But he's awfully polite about it."

Mrs. Rosenwald still keeps what she calls the Vice-President's all purpose "TFX speech," named for the fighter plane (later dubbed F-111), that former Defense Secretary McNamara dreamed would replace all other military airplanes. It can be used—with the deletion of a paragraph here, the insertion of another there, under just about any circumstance. It has four main themes: peace, inflation, law and order, and urban problems. Any one can be emphasized, depending upon the audience; the others may be played down, or eliminated entirely.

Cynthia Rosenwald was catapulted into the limelight after Agnew's New Orleans speech denouncing "effete snobs." Ironically—or so she claims—that was one of the few in which she had absolutely no part.

"My husband says I'm the only person ever to become a national figure because of something I didn't do," she says.

Cynthia began getting press coverage of her own.

"In Annapolis, all the press gang knew her," Thompson says now. "It was 'Hi, Cindy.' . . . 'How's it going, Cindy?' . . . 'Have a drink with us later, gal.' But no one wrote about her, and that was how she liked it."

One day she came to work and there were the crew and an announcer from a national television network, cameras set up, waiting outside her office door. Cindy had driven over from Baltimore, parked her car on a fringe parking lot, and ridden a bus to work.

"She panicked," Thompson grins. "She absolutely panicked."

For a long time she wouldn't see anyone from the press. I left my number ten days in a row; she never returned my call. When we finally met in Thompson's office she was still as nervous as a cat on ice.

The task President Nixon has given Agnew as head of a Cabinet committee to supervise integration of Southern school districts may turn out to be the toughest he has tackled.

He makes no bones that he disagrees—strongly disagrees— with the Supreme Court's decision in the Alexander case ordering Mississippi school districts to desegregate "forthwith." His Jackson speech is proof enough of that. In private, he speaks even more harshly about it. That immediate desegregation was ordered into effect February 1, 1970, when the court could have as easily waited for another term to begin in September, he regards as cruel and unnecessary.

Yet he fully intends to support it.

"We are all trying to live under a system of laws and representative government," he said on TV. "It is ridiculous to be an advocate of law and order in one sense and attempt to circumvent it in another."

Nixon had been ready to announce formation of the committee, to be chaired by the Vice-President, at his televised news conference on the evening of January 30. But no questions about civil rights were asked. So he let Agnew announce it in a Sunday panel show on February 1.

"Through discussion and dialogue," the Vice-President said, "we will work to achieve the spirit and the letter of the court decision in ways that will least impair the continuance of quality education in those districts."

That will probably make him enemies on both sides. The liberals and the militants already have written him off. Many parents, fearful for their children's education and even their physical safety, will blame him for not being able to reverse the Supreme Court, turn back a decision that he, as a lawyer and a father, feels is wrong.

Agnew says his daughter Pamela taught school until she married. (Pamela went back to the Towson Presbyterian Church to marry her childhood sweetheart, Robert De- Haven, on June 21, 1969. President and Mrs. Nixon were guests. The couple now live on Maryland's Eastern Shore where DeHaven teaches handicapped children.) Agnew says Pamela quit teaching because she could not maintain order, let alone impart knowledge.

"And that," he observed, "was not a ghetto district. These

were middle-class white students. They had no discipline. That's the permissive spirit of the age in which we live, unfortunately."

In one sense, Agnew is probably the most primitive—to use that term to denote lack of subterfuge—man ever to be Vice-President. He has never learned the reasons for ducking a question; he has yet to be convinced that a soft answer is to be preferred over a direct one.

His friends are of the same order. When he went to Maryland to speak after his return from the Far East, the Baltimore papers were on strike. Most politicians, including those who had fought with the papers, would either ignore the strike or profess to be distressed. Agnew said cheerily that this was his favorite time of the year to visit Maryland—"When the papers are on strike." The audience whooped.

Strangely enough, Agnew was friendly with former President Lyndon B. Johnson, a Democrat, as Johnson's term drew to a close. "The press was trying to get me to say something it could use against Johnson and the war," Agnew said, revealing once again his distrust of the media. "And I wouldn't."

Johnson must have heard about it, because Agnew thereafter was a frequent guest at White House dinners.

After Agnew's election, Johnson gave him this bit of advice: "Young man, we have in this country two big television networks, NBC and CBS. We have two news magazines, *Newsweek* and *Time*. We have two wire services, AP and UPI. We have two pollsters, Gallup and Harris. We have two big newspapers—The *Washington Post* and *The New York Times*. They're all so damned big they think they own the country. But, young man, don't get any ideas about fighting them. Because they come out daily, and you don't."

This was advice Agnew rejected. He has not hesitated to fight them.

Agnew rates his Far Eastern trip—which took him to eleven countries—his biggest success. He believes it is a story never fully told; in Taiwan, for instance, President Chiang Kai-shek insisted on driving him to the airport so they could continue their discussions. In country after country, he feels he allayed fears, built confidence in the United States. Perhaps the story is too big to be told at one time.

What has given him his greatest satisfaction?

His Des Moines speech in which he tore into television. He enjoyed that thoroughly. Millions of people saw and heard it, they did not have to rely on someone else to tell them what he had said.

Part of his trouble on the campaign trail, he feels, was that most newspapers and wire services assigned second-echelon reporters to his party.

On his Far Eastern trip, he says, he had first-string reporters with him and "you could tell the difference." Despite his political difficulties with *The New York Times*, he pays grudging respect to its writers. Agnew has had five *Times* men with him—"one was a Negro who hated my guts as an individual"—but they never let that interfere with their reporting—"They played it right down the middle, and I honor them for it."

One of the unexpected dividends of his Vice-Presidency, he says, has been the Secret Service men assigned to protect him around the clock. There are thirty-five in all, working three eight-hour shifts, all young, bright, physically fit, and dedicated.

"They've become like members of the family," he says. "Judy says she feels like a house mother."

The Agnew party returned from its Far Eastern trip at five P.M. on January 19, 1970. There were the usual airport greetings and speeches, and then they went home to the Sheraton Park. The Secret Service detail that had accompanied them went home at midnight, and another came on duty.

The Agnews, however, had been through too many time changes. They had crossed the International Dateline. They were disoriented.

Sleepless at 1:30 A.M., Agnew turned on the light and looked over at his wife. She was wide-awake. "This is ridiculous," he said. "I'm going to get up and pay the bills."

He had forgotten that he now had a housekeeper whose job it was to write the checks. She had locked up all the bills.

He picked up the phone and called the Secret Service detail in the hotel command post. "What time is it?" he asked.

"It's 1:50," an agent named Bill (Secret Service men do not like to have their identity disclosed) replied. "Who in the hell is this?"

"The Vice-President."

"Oh"—a long pause—"you can't sleep, sir?"

"Never mind. Good night."

"Good night, sir."

Mrs. Agnew was up now.

"Why not fix breakfast?" he asked.

At 2:30 A.M. she prepared bacon, eggs, coffee, and toast. They ate in silence.

"Are you coming to bed now?" she asked.

Agnew still wasn't sleepy. "I'm going to work," he said, and called for his limousine.

That morning he arrived at the Executive Office Building at 3:50 A.M. He has not let his staff forget it.

Agnew had a lot of catching up to do. There were reports on his Far Eastern trip—to the President, to the National Security Council, to congressional committees.

And there were councils and committees he heads whose work cound not go much further until he had made vital decisions.

In Washington, a great deal of the Vice-President's time is taken up with the jobs President Nixon has given him.

Some of these demand more time than others.

He devotes relatively little time to the President's Council on Physical Fitness, directed now by Astronaut James Lovell in a line of succession that includes football coach Bud Wilkinson and Baseball Hall of Famer Stan Musial, because its program is well set and functioning smoothly.

He devotes considerably more time to the President's Council on Youth Opportunity, directed by Henry Shine. He intends to expand it from a summer recreation program into a yearlong project that will involve training in job skills.

Until its report was sent to the White House in September, 1969, he worked long hours with the Council on Space and Technology, whose mission was to set the nation's space goals after Apollo.

His performance in convening the first session of the National Council on Indian Opportunity in the two years since it was set up by former President Johnson, won the grudging approval of LaDonna Harris, whose husband, Senator Fred Harris of Oklahoma, was the Democratic National Chairman at that time. Mrs. Harris, a Comanche, is one of six Indian members.

Together they presented what she called a "grocery list" of demands, including the creation of an assistant secretaryship of Interior for Indian affairs to a "massive infusion of funds" for Indian education.

Vice-President Agnew instructed the Secretaries of Interior, Agriculture, Commerce, Labor, Housing and Urban Development, Health, Education and Welfare, as well as the director of the office of Economic Opportunity to report within thirty days whether the government had the means to honor the recommendations. He said it was "outrageous" that Indians are the most poverty-stricken of Americans and said the Nixon administration would aim its attack at "that raw truth."

Even more impressive, however, was the way he handled the meeting. The Indians were allowed to speak first—ahead, even, of any Cabinet officer. Like most minority groups, Indians can be rather sensitive about such matters. They often feel they are being dictated, rather than listened, to. That the council met at all was a step forward.

Agnew, had had his first contact with American Indians earlier, at a convention of the Congress of American Indians in Albuquerque, New Mexico, on October 8, 1969. Secretary of the Interior Walter Hickel and Indian Affairs Commissioner Louis R. Bruce had been heckled by a small group of militants. Agnew got a warmer reception. Congress President Walter Chino called his remarks, which promised a new deal to Indians, a "positive statement."

But the Albuquerque meeting also gave Agnew one of those opportunities he so dearly loves—a chance to mix work and politics.

Senator Edward M. Kennedy (D.-Mass.) had spoken at the meeting the day before the Vice-President. He had annoyed Agnew with charges that the Nixon policy toward Indians was "a national failure of major proportions."

En route to Albuquerque, Agnew rewrote a part of his speech and later telephoned it back to Herb Thompson in Washington to be sure that Kennedy read it.

> When I prepared these remarks [he said], I saw no advantage in placing blame for the present situation.
>
> However, Senator Kennedy's insinuations of yesterday require some response.
>
> Yesterday, Senator Kennedy described the government's Indian policy as a national failure of major proportions. I would have to agree that these policies have been less than effective.

However, I must remind you that Senator Kennedy's party presided over these failures for the past eight years—eight years of Democratic control of the White House and a Democratic-controlled Congress.

This makes it difficult for me to understand what the senator means when he says "No more buck passing" . . . "We need no more promises . . . we know they are empty."

The one thing that the senator did say that I understand is his statement that "we know where the blame lies. . . . It lies in eight years of inaction, crocodile tears, and fancy promises by the same people who now send Senator Kennedy here to commiserate with you.

Each of the councils and committees the Vice-President heads has its own director and staff. Nils Boe, former Republican governor of South Dakota, for instance, heads the Office of Inter-Governmental Relations and has a suite directly across the hall from the Vice-President's.

His own Vice-Presidential staff is comparatively small. Most of its members work out of the Executive Office Building. Walter Mote, a veteran Republican figure on Capitol Hill, holds down his congressional office with the title of assistant to the president of the Senate.

Stan Blair, lawyer and gentleman farmer from Harford County, Maryland,—"named after the bastard son of Lord Baltimore but that no longer applies"—is his chief of staff. Their offices are separated only by a carpeted waiting room, presided over by Alice Fringer.

Blair and Agnew first met in 1965 when Agnew was Baltimore County executive and Blair was a delegate to the Maryland General Assembly. Agnew appeared before the assembly's revenue committees, of which Blair was a member.

When Agnew ran for governor and won, Blair was the Republican candidate against State Senator William James, now president of the state senate, and lost. Agnew called him a few days later and asked him to drop by for a conference. Blair was not ready to retire from public life, and secretary of state in Agnew's state cabinet was one of the jobs he wanted. When Agnew offered it he accepted. When Agnew went to Washington, Blair followed.

Agnew's professional staff is heavily loaded with Marylanders. It includes: C.D. Ward, assistant for domestic affairs, one-time general counsel for the National Association of

County Officials: Jerome Wolff, special assistant for science
and technology, Agnew's chairman of the Maryland State
Roads Commission; Arthur Sohmer, special assistant for political affairs, Agnew's chief political adviser in Annapolis;
Dr. Jean Spencer, special assistant for research, a University
of Maryland professor; Ernst Minor, schedule and appointments secretary, a Cleveland, Ohio, radio station owner;
Frank De Costa, special assistant for human relations, a
former Maryland assistant attorney general; Kent Crane,
special assistant for foreign affairs, career Foreign Service
officer on loan from the State Department; Herbert Thompson, press secretary, formerly Associated Press bureau chief
in Annapolis; and Colonel Michael Dunn, military aide, a
career Army officer.

The names of these men and women are largely unknown
to most of the American people. But these men and women,
like their boss, are one heartbeat away from the Presidency
and could, in an emergency, take over the machinery of
government and become, like him, household words.

Much has been said of late about the "new Agnew." When
did he change from liberal to conservative? Why?

Governor McKeldin says he has not changed. Agnew and
his closest friends swear he hasn't.

A study of his speeches as governor seem to bear this out.
Those who insist he has "changed"—motivated by personal
pique or injured pride, explanations that do him no honor—
simply haven't read the record.

When rioting broke out in Cambridge, on Maryland's
Eastern Shore, in July, 1967, Agnew went there and walked
the streets to see for himself what was happening. On the
evening of July 24 he went to his summer cottage in Ocean
City, wrote this statement and telephoned it to Thompson in
Annapolis for release to the press:

> In Maryland, rioting or inciting to riot, no matter what
> wrong is said to be the cause, will not be tolerated. There
> are proper ways to protest and they must be used. It shall
> now be the policy of this state to immediately arrest any
> person inciting to riot, and to not allow that person to
> finish his vicious speech. All lawbreakers will be vigorously
> and promptly prosecuted.
>
> Acts of violence will not be later forgiven just because the
> criminal after a while adopts a more reasonable attitude. The
> violent cannot be allowed to sneak unnoticed from the war

dance to the problem-solving meeting. The problem-solving conference must be reserved for those who shun lawlessness, who win their place at the conference table by leadership that builds rather than destroys.

The problem-solving must be done by constructive militants, such as the [Roy] Wilkinses, [Martin Luther] Kings, and [A. Philip] Randolphs—not by the [Stokely] Carmichaels and [Rap] Browns. But it should include the younger, responsible leadership as well as the older, more established, leaders. Responsibility is the yardstick.

It shall continue to be my firm policy to do everything possible to provide jobs, good housing, and better educational opportunities for the poor and underprivileged, both Negro and white, in Maryland. I will meet with any responsible leaders to discuss the problems that confront us. I will *not* meet with those who engage in, or urge, riots or other criminal acts as weapons to obtain power.

In conclusion, I commend the citizens of both races who have continued to conduct themselves with intelligent restraint in spite of great pressure. I share the sorrow of those who have suffered and who continue to suffer from the reckless acts of a few.

For the confused and the weak who seek to excuse, appease, or rationalize for the criminals who threaten our society I have only pity.

This was nine months before he ordered the arrest of 227 Bowie State College students who conducted a sit-in at the state capital, demanding that the governor meet with them, and nine months before he clashed publicly with established Negro leaders in Baltimore for denouncing extremists to both races.

In an address to the thirty-eighth annual convention of the New Jersey Federation of Republican Women at Atlantic City on May 8, 1968, Governor Agnew said:

Principle—like patriotism—is an old-fashioned word that seems destined for the graveyard. . . . Who needs to bother with means or methods as long as ends are achieved? Who needs to condemn civil disobedience until it leads to civil disorder? . . .

The American dream is turning into the American nightmare. The heroic American has turned into the anxious American. The bread and circus programs of the Great Society, like those of the once great Roman Republic, seem to drain the vigor from our spirit.

. . . What good are revolutions if we are devoured by them? For how long can mere innovation masquerade as substance? . . . Are we to remain a nation of sheep led by Judas goats down the paths of deception and self-destruction? . . . We are a people bereft of inspiration and adrift without policy. The confidence of the American people that once could conquer a continent has been shaken to the core. We cower before the challenges we face, we cringe where once we would tower. . . .

Sound familiar?

And two days later, before a conference on police and community relationships in Baltimore, he said:

. . . defiance of law allows cynical leaders responsible to none to exploit the madness of the mob. Rapidly, civil disobedience falls prey to civil disorder. Passive resistance gives way to erosive force. Logical leadership is obscured by the demagogue's harangue.

This phenomenon is apparent in our cities and on our college campuses where his ideals have disintegrated and legitimate causes have disappeared. And while no thinking person denies that social injustice exists, no thinking person can condone any group, for any reason, taking justice in his own hands. Once this is permitted, democracy dies; for democracy is sustained through one great premise: the premise that civil rights are balanced by civil responsibilities.

That was Agnew as governor. But few heard. When he spoke to a nation, it listened, with disbelief, horror—or hope.

Agnew has not suffered as bad a press as he thinks. But the point is, he thinks so.

"I don't quarrel with anyone who disagrees with me," he says, for once a bit pompously. "What burns me up"—he continues, becoming himself again—"is this organized effort to give me an image that is totally false, unlike anything I've ever been, simply by repeating the stories they've concocted over and over again."

One story he does not intend to repudiate is his campaign statement—greeted with moral outrage by many—"When you've seen one slum you've seen them all."

He and Herb Thompson can't agree where the remark was

made. Thompson insists it was on a TV show in Detroit and he has the tape—if only he could find it. Agnew thinks it was at a press conference in "some hotel"—he remembers very clearly—and thinks it might have been Minneapolis.

At any rate, he said it. He sticks by it.

"You don't gain more insight into human problems," he says, "by going time after time to look at rotten buildings no human ought to be required to live in, pay exorbitant rents on. Slums are engraved on my consciousness. But in my dictionary, slums are buildings and conditions, not people. My remark was twisted, warped, to make it appear that I am indifferent to human misery."

Dr. Gilbert Ware says Agnew could never understand Negro militants. The more he saw and heard of them, the wider the gulf became.

There is a lot of truth in that. Agnew is appalled not only by the militants, but by what he calls their kid-glove treatment in the media. When he went to Baltimore to speak recently, members of an organization called the Friends of the Black Panthers turned out in force. The press called their demonstration "peaceful."

"Peaceful?" Agnew asks in total disbelief. "There were my wife and daughters getting out of the car, and those people were screaming at the tops of their voices: 'F---you, Agnew! F---you, Agnew!' That's peaceful?"

Agnew believes the black ghettos can be rebuilt and made viable, and that black capitalism is the answer. Goods and services must be sold in the ghetto and the Negro should be the one to market them. But he has no patience with those who want everything "on a silver platter" day before yesterday. He contrasts their irrationality with the good sense of the American Indians who are willing to settle for half a loaf for the time being, if they can't have a whole one. He obviously likes the Indians and intends to help them.

"I was talking to Maurie Stans (Maurice Stans, Secretary of Commerce) this morning," he once told me. "He says we will have one hundred black-owned firms in our ghettos, with a capital investment of three-hundred million dollars by the middle of the year. We have forty now. That's progress.

"Negroes now own five percent of the major franchises. That will go up to fifteen percent in five years. And that is progress. But you never hear about it. This administration will never get credit for anything it does for the black man."

The press of business has restricted Agnew's golf game and

he has turned to tennis. There are courts on the White House grounds, but he and his partners prefer those at the Naval Observatory. He usually plays with C. D. Ward, of his own staff, Postmaster-General Winston Blount, Labor Secretary George Schultz, Senator Charles Percy (R.-Ill.), or Bryce Harlow, of the White House staff.

When he is in California, he sometimes plays at Dinah Shore's home. Ward, a bachelor, is White House adviser Henry Kissinger's only rival as the Nixon administration "swinger." He dates Miss Shore occasionally.

But Agnew prefers work.

"If he had to choose between getting his teeth into a policy matter of major importance and going out to a political gathering to make a few innocuous remarks, he'd stay back and wrestle with policy," Blair says.

Agnew sometimes returns from TV appearances complaining about "stupid questions."

"The kind my boss wants to have thrown at him," says Cynthia Rosenwald, "would be something like: 'Equate the political-economic differential between MIRV and SALT.' He has all this vast store of information inside him, and he wants to share it."

He still likes to get in his licks at those who have tried to humiliate him. At a private dinner in New York he was asked to explain why he had so little rapport with the "intellectual community."

"In the first place," Agnew said slowly, "I do not think there is an intellectual community in this country. If there is one, I don't think it's limited to one area. Those who claim to be are invariably self-nominated and self-elected; they are visceral, rather than intellectual, in their reactions. I would prefer to think that we have a vast body of well-informed people who are too busy to care whether they are considered intellectuals or not."

How does he see the future? Does he believe this country is Plato's degenerating Republic?

"I think," he says, "we have arrested the trend. We've had a more peaceful year.

"But the time has come to demand self-discipline.

"It is time, if necessary, to risk being unpopular."

INDEX

AFL-CIO, 19

Abrams, Al, 66

Acceptance of Vice Presidential Nomination, 84-5

Acheson, Dean, 39

Aganost, 11

Agnew, Elinor Isobel, (Judy), 23, 44, 48-50, 51, 65, 87, 88, 103, 111, 133, 134, 144, 145
  Parents, 14

Agnew, James Rand, (Randy), 16, 43, 44, 50, 71, 87

Agnew, Kim, 43, 44, 71, 87, 100, 109

Agnew Mystique, 9, 137

Agnew, Pamela, 16, 43, 44, 71, 88, 142-3

Agnew, Spiro Theodore
  Acceptance of Vice Presidential Nomination, 84-5
  Anti-Ballistic Missiles, 114
  Army Career
    Korean War, 17
    World War II, 15-6
  Baltimore County Executive, 10, 13, 22, 25, 26, 31-6
  Birthplace, 9, 11
  Business Career, 14-9
  Campaign Song, 51
  Campaign Trail, 88-100
  Charges against during Vice Presidential Campaign, 93-4
  Children, 16, 43, 44, 50, 71, 87, 88, 100, 109, 142-3
  Civil Rights Program, 34
  Committee to Supervise Integration of Southern School Districts, 137, 142
  Decision to Support Nixon, 69

Draft Rockefeller Movement, 64-7

Education, 12, 13, 14, 16

Election Results, 1968 Presidential, 100

Family History, 9-11

First Year as Governor of Maryland, 44-51

Governor of Maryland, 26, 35, 37-62

Gubernatorial Campaign, 37-44

Health, 132-3

Inauguration, Governor of Maryland, 44

Income Tax, 34, 45

Inlaws, 14

Joins Democratic Party, 17

Joins Republican Party, 17

Labor Lawyer, 24-7

Legal Career, 19-27

Marriage, 15

National Council on Indian Opportunity, 105, 136, 145-7

Nomination for Vice President, 77-83

Nomination Speech, Nixon for President, 70, 73-6

Offices of the Vice President, 136

PTA President, 23

Personal Friends, 134-5

Pollution, 45

Prison Reform, 46

Public Kindergarten, 34

Social Life, 133

Southeast Asian Tour, 106, 134, 143-4

Space Program, 25, 105

Sports
  Golf, 36, 70, 138, 151

153

Tennis, 132
State Constitution, 61-2
Student Protest, 52-4
Tugboat Strike, 51
Typical Day of the Vice President, 135-6
Urban Renewal, 34, 45
Vice Presidential Campaign, 13, 77-100
Views on Vice Presidency, 105
Zoning Board, 27
Agnew, Susan, 44, 48, 71, 88
Agnew, Theodore Spiro, 9-13, 14
Akers, Margaret, 11
Amalgamated Meat Cutters and Butcher Workmen of North America, AFL-CIO, 19, 24, 51
American Civil Liberties Union, 123
American Nazi Party, 57, 121
Anagnostopoulous Family, 10
Anderson, Dale, 33
Anti-ballistic Missile Bases, 114
Arends, Leslie, 136
Armetta, Charles, 135
Army Career
  Korean War, 17
  World War II, 15-6

Baker, Howard, 125
Ball, John, 25
Baltimore Colts, 35-6
Baltimore County Executive, 10, 13, 22, 25, 26, 31-6
Baltimore County Zoning Board of Appeals, 27
Baltimore News-American, 61, 69
Baltimore Orioles, 36
Baltimore Sun, 42, 45, 46, 47, 51, 68, 90, 97, 99, 128, 134
Baltimore University, 14, 16, 32
Barret, E. Lester, 17, 19, 30, 31, 23, 30, 35, 70, 109, 133
Bascom, Marion C., 60
Battle of the Bulge, 16

Battle of the Peanut Butter Jars, 49
Beall, J. Glenn, Jr., 67
Beichman, Arnold, 130
Berry, George M., 9
Birmingham, Michael, 29-32
Birthplace, 9, 11
Black Dispatch, The, 57
Blair, C. Stanley, 47, 136, 139, 147, 152
Blount, Winston, 152
Boe, Nils, 147
Bowie State College, 52, 61, 149
Bressler, Charles, 87
Brewster, Daniel, 62
Brighton Restaurant, 11
Brinkley, David, 123, 124
Brown, H. Rap, 57, 58, 149
Buchanan, Patrick, 71
Burch, Francis, 46
Business Career, 14-9
Butler, John Marshall, 36
Byrd, H. C., 37

Cain, Anne, 49
Camp Croft, 15
Campaign Song, 51
Campaign Trail, Vice Presidential, 88-100
Canzanni, Joseph, 135
Carmichael, Stokely, 56, 57, 58, 121, 149
Carroll, Joseph, 57
Cavanaugh, Jerome, 125
Charges Against Agnew During Vice Presidential Campaign, 93-4
Chesaco Inn, 13
Chiang Kai-shek, 143
Children, 16, 43, 44, 50, 71, 87, 88, 100, 109, 142-3
Citizen's Task Force on Space, 25
Civil Rights, 34, 38, 86
Civil Rights Record, 86
Clark, Bob, 92
Cleaver, Eldridge, 122
Coffin, Jonathan, 47
Committee to Supervise Integration of Southern School Districts, 137, 142

Constitution, State of Maryland, 61-2
Cooper, Paul, 47
Council on Space and Technology, 136, 145
Council on Urban Affairs, 105
Crane, Kent, 148
Crawford, Clare, 49, 111
Cronkite, Walter, 123, 124

D'Alessandro, Thomas, 60
Davison Chemical Company, 14
Decision to Support Nixon, 69
DeCosta, Frank, 148
DeFlippio, Frank, 47, 69
DeHaven, Robert, 142
Democratic Party
  Baltimore County Executive, 28-33
  Candidate for Governor of Maryland, 26
  History in Baltimore County, 28
  Investigating in Towson, 92
  Presidential Election Results, 1968, 100
  Presidential Nominee, 89, 95
  Ratio in Baltimore County, 21
  Spiro Agnew as Member, 17
  State Legislature, 45
  Theodore Agnew as member, 10, 12, 14
Depression Years, 11, 13
Devereaux, James, 30, 34-5
Dewey, Thomas E., 79
Dirksen, Everett, 79, 90, 114
Dixon, Willard, 57
Draft Rockefeller Movement, 64-7
Dunn, Michael, 148

Education, 12, 13, 14, 16
Edwards, Xavier, 41
Effete Snobs, 48, 109-11, 115, 116
Eisenhower, Dwight D., 73, 98
Election Results, 1968 Presidential, 100
Elizabethtown, Kentucky, 16
Eney, H. Vernon, 61

Environmental Quality Council, 105
Ethnic Remarks, 90-2
Evans, Daniel J., 73
Evening Sunpaper, 47
Evers, Charles, 125

Face the Nation, 136
Family History, 9-11
Fannin, Paul, 79
Finch, Robert, 137
Finin, Thomas, 36, 37-9, 42
First Year as Governor of Maryland, 44
Fiscal Reform, 45
Ford, Jerry, 136
Forest Park High School, 12
Fort Knox, 15
Franklin, Ben, 97-9
Friends of the Black Panthers, 151
Fringer, Alice, 67, 140, 147

Gargalianos, Messenia, Greece, 10
Garrison Junior High School, 12
Gleitsmann, Carl, 18
Goldstein, Leonard, 123
Goldstein, Louis, 46, 100
Goldwater, Barry, 63, 73, 79
Golf, 36, 70, 138, 151
Goodell, Charles, 114, 138
Goodman, Julian, 122
Goodman, Robert, 140
Gore, Albert, 65, 115
Gore, Louise, 65
Governor of Maryland, 26, 35, 37-62
Goucher College, 20
Graham, Billy, 79, 137
Graham, Katherine, 128, 129
Greek Background, 10
Griffin, Robert, 136
Grogg, Lester L., 21-2
Gubernatorial Campaign, 37-44

Hague, Frank, 29
Halderman, H. R., 71
Hammond, Hall, 44

Hanson, Royce, 39
Hardesty, Edward, 27, 33-4
Hardin, Nancy, 132
Harlow, Bryce, 114, 137, 152
Harriman, Averill, 110, 116, 120-1, 125
Harris, Fred, 145-6
Harris, LaDonna, 145-6
Hatfield, Mark, 78
Helms, Richard, 87
He's My Kind of Man, Ted Agnew Is, (Campaign Song), 51
Hinman, George, 66
History of the Vice Presidency, 100-5
Hook, Sidney, 130
Hoover, J. Edgar, 37
Hope, Bob, 138
Howard University, 52
Huebner, Lee, 123-4
Humphrey, Hubert, 89, 95, 99, 100, 101, 126

Inauguration, Governor of Maryland, 44
Income Tax, 34, 45
Indians, 105, 136, 145-7, 151
Inlaws, 14
Integration, 38, 42, 59, 137, 142

Jacobs, Brad, 20, 45
Javits, Jacob, 76, 81
John Birch Society, 57, 90
Johns Hopkins University, 14
Johnson, Lyndon B., 68, 87, 101, 103, 143
Judefind, Elinor Isabel, (Judy), 14
Judefind, W. Lee, 14

Kahl, Christian H., 29-31, 32, 140
Kennedy, Edward, 116, 120, 146
Kennedy, John F., 42, 101, 103
Kerrigan, Thomas, 25
Kimmel, Sam, 9, 21, 23, 24, 26, 32, 133
Kindergarten, 34

King, Martin Luther, Jr., 54, 57, 149
Kissinger, Henry, 152
Korean War, 17-8
Kristol, Irving, 130
Ku Klux Klan, 41, 61
Ky, Nguyen Cau, 50

Labor Lawyer, 24-7
Lacquer, Walter, 130
Lane, William Preston, Jr., 37, 45
Law Partner, 9
Legal Career, 19-27
Life, 127
Lindsay, James J., 9
Lindsay, John, 73, 78, 80, 81-3
Lippmann, Walter, 122
Loch Raven
  Inter-Community Association, 23
  Kiwanis, 23
  PTA, 23, 32
Lovell, James, 145
Lumberman Mutual Insurance Co., 17
Luperini, Sabatino, 135
Lutherville, Maryland, 19
Lynch, Connie, 57

Mahoney, George, 26, 36, 37-44
Mandel, Marvin, 46, 47, 103, 134
Marriage, 15
Maryland
  Constitution, 61-2
  First Year as Governor, 44-51
  Governor, 26, 35, 37-62
  Gubernatorial Campaign, 37-44
  Inauguration, 44
  Pollution, 45
  Prison Reform, 46
  Tax Reform, 45
  Tugboat Strike, 51
  Urban Renewal, 34, 45
Maryland Casualty Co., 14
Mathias, Charles Mac, 36, 66
Matsanuga, Sparks, 91
McCarthy, Eugene, 101

McGee, Frank, 124
McKeldin, Theodore Roosevelt, 17, 19, 36, 45, 62, 63, 148
Meet the Press, 65
Menchine, Albert W., 9, 13
Menhadden Fishermen, 25
Miami Beach, 9
   Republican National Convention 1968, 70-87
Minor, Ernst, 148
Mitchell, Clarence, Jr., 86
Mitchell, John N., 132, 137
Mitchell, Martha, 132
Montgomery County Sentinel, 50
Moore, E. Scott, 21, 31
Morgan State College, 41
Morton, Rodgers C. B., 36, 80, 81
Moser, Herbert, 19
Mote, Walter, 147
Moynihan, Daniel Patrick, 137
Mudd, Roger, 125
Musial, Stan, 145
Muskie, Edmund, 89, 100, 114, 125
Myers, Samuel, 52

National Aeronautics and Space Council, 105
National Council on Indian Opportunity, 105, 136, 145-7
National Council on Marine Resources and Engineering Development, 105
National Security Council, 105, 136, 145
Negro
   Black Capitalism, 151
   College Students, 52
   Integration, 137, 142
   Martin Luther King, Jr., 54
   Menhadden Fishermen, 25
   Militants, 151
   Public Kindergarten, 34
   Racism in Gubernatorial Campaign, 41
   Reaction to Nomination, 87
   Reaction to Speech to Leaders, 60
   Relationship with, 18

Rioting in Cambridge, 148-9
Riots in Baltimore, 54
Strike in Courtland, Virginia, 26
Struggle for Urban Renewal, 34
Nelson, Gaylord, 125
New York Post, 18
New York Times, The, 18, 28, 48, 80, 92, 95, 97-100, 106, 109, 121, 126, 127, 128-31, 143, 144
News-American, 47
Newsweek, 78, 128, 143
Nixon, Richard M.
   Agnew's Decision to Support Nixon, 69
   Agnew's Nominating Speech, August 7, 1968, 70, 73-6
   Appoints Agnew to Head Committee on Integration, 137, 142
   Arrival at Miami National Convention, 1968, 72-3
   Assignment of Space Program, 25
   Chooses Agnew as Running Mate, 77-83
   Decision for Running Mate, 9
   Defends Agnew, 98
   Faith in Agnew, 132
   First Meetings with Agnew, 65
   Guest at Wedding of Pamela Agnew, 142
   Inauguration, 50
   New York Lunch with Agnew, 68
   Nomination for President, 73-6
   Presidential Election Results, 1968, 100
   TV Reaction to State of the Union Message, 125-6
   Vietnamization Program, 138
   Views on Vice Presidency, 105
   Nomination for Vice Presidency, 77-83
   Nomination Speech, Nixon for President, 1968, 70; 73-6
Novak, Robert, 125

O'Connor, Herbert, 37
Office of Intergovernmental Re-
    lations, 105, 136, 147
Offutt, Tom, 21
Ogilvie, Richard, 79, 81
Oishi, Gene, 89-92
Open Housing, 38, 42, 59
Oursler, George, 17

PTA, 23, 32
Patton, George S., Jr., 16
Peace Corps National Advisory
    Council, 105
Peanut Butter Jars, Battle of, 49
Pearl Harbor, 15
Pegler, Westbrook, 128
Pemberton, John deJ., Jr., 123
Pendergast, Tom, 29
Pepersack, Vernon L., 46
Percy, Charles, 78, 80, 152
Physician, 132
Picadilly Restaurant, 11
Pollard, W. Roy, 11
Pollard, William, 11
Pollution, 45
Power, Henry, 134
Power, Hugh, 134
President's Council on Physical
    Fitness and Sports, 105,
    145
President's Council on Youth
    Opportunity, 105, 136,
    145
Pressman, Hyman A., 40, 42
Price, Ray, 71
Prison System Reform, 46
Professional Staff, 147-8
Proxmire, William, 115
Public Kindergarten, 34
Public School No. 69, 12

Queen, Emmett, 132, 134

Racism
    Gubernatorial Campaign, 41
    Speech to Negro Leaders, 54-
    60
Randolph, A. Philip, 149
Rather, Dan, 124, 125

Reagan, Ronald, 72, 76, 78
Republican Party
    Agnew Joined, 17
    Candidate for Baltimore
        County Executive, 31-3
    Candidate for Governor of
        Maryland, 26, 36
    Governors' Conference, De-
        cember, 1969, 113-4
    Presidental Election Results,
        1968, 100
    National Convention, Miami,
        1968, 70-87
    Ratio in Baltimore County,
        21
Restaurants, of Theodore Agnew
    Brighton, 11
    Chesaco Inn, 13
    Picadilly, 11
Reston, James, 128
Rhodes, James A., 70, 79
Rioting, Statement on, 148-9
Ripon Society, 123
Rockefeller, Nelson, 64-9, 70, 76
    Draft Rockefeller Movement,
        64-7
Rockwell, George Lincoln, 121
Rogers, Douglas, 132
Rogers Forge PTA, 23, 32
Romney, George, 64, 67, 70, 72,
        78, 81, 84
Roosevelt, Franklin D., 13, 103
Roosevelt, Theodore, 102
Rosenwald, Cynthia, 138, 139-
        42, 152
Rosenwald, Peter, 138
Rudd, Hughes, 71
Rusk, Dean, 87

St. Louis Globe Democrat, 99
Sasscer, Lansdale, 37
Savage, Phillip, 87
Schacter, Leon, 24, 25, 26
Schreiber Brothers, 18, 24
Scott, Hugh, 136
Scranton, William, 64
Secret Service, 79, 88, 104, 135,
        144
Severeid, Eric, 124, 125
Shine, Henry, 145
Shore, Dinah, 152

Sickles, Carleton, 26, 36, 37-9
Silent Majority, 113, 138
Skouras, Spyros, 13
Slaten, Roy, 45
Slot Machine Interests, 41
Smith and Barnet, 16, 17
Smith, Ken, 135
Smith, Michael Paul, 17, 19
Sohmer, Arthur, 87, 148
Space Program, 25, 105
Speeches
    January 25, 1967, Inaugural
        Address as Governor of
        Maryland, 44-5
    April, 1968, To Negro Lead-
        ers of Maryland, 54-60
    April, 1968, New Haven,
        Conn., First for Rocke-
        feller, 65
    May 8, 1968, Atlantic City,
        N. J., Civil Disobedience,
        149-50
    May 10, 1968, Baltimore,
        Md., Civil Disobedience,
        150
    August 7, 1968, Miami Beach,
        Fla., Nominating Nixon,
        70, 73-6
    August 8, 1968, Miami Beach,
        Fla., Acceptance of Vice
        Presidential Nomination,
        84-5
    June 7, 1969, Ohio State Uni-
        versity Commencement,
        Effetism, 112-3
    October 19, 1969, Effete
        Snobs, 109-11
    October 20, 1969, Jackson,
        Miss., Youth and Civil
        Rights, 117-8
    October 30, 1969, Harrisburg,
        Penna., Impudence in the
        Streets, 116-7
    November 10, 1969, Philadel-
        phia, Penna., In Defense
        of America's Values,
        118-20
    November 13, 1969, Des
        Moines, Iowa, Attack on
        the TV Networks, 120-2,
        144
    November 29, 1969, Mont-
        gomery, Ala., Power of
        the Press, 127-31
    December, 1969, Hawaii, Si-
        lent Majority, 113
    December, 1969, Quotes from
        Southeast Asia Tour,
        106-8
    Method of Writing, 139-44
    Total in 1969, 139
Speechwriter, 138
Spencer, Jean, 148
Sports
    Golf, 36, 70, 138, 151
    Tennis, 152
Stans, Maurice, 151
Stanton, Frank, 123, 124
Steinbock, Charles, Jr., 93
Steinmann, Karl, 19
Strickland, Frank, 23, 24, 32,
    34, 36
Student Protest, 52-4
Sulzberger, Arthur Ochs, 129

Tallmer, Jerry, 18
Tawes, J. Millard, 30, 34, 37,
    42, 45, 61, 62
Tax Reform, 45
Tennis, 152
Thompson, Herb, 47, 49, 60, 66,
    68, 87, 137, 141, 148,
    150
Thurmond, Strom, 79, 80
Time, 111, 143
Times, Gowrie, Iowa, 131
Tour of Southeast Asia, 106,
    134, 143-4
Towson Jeffersonian, 23, 31, 32
Towson, Maryland, 9, 19, 20,
    92, 97
Towson State College, 20
Towson Times, 31
Truman, Harry, 18, 103
Tugboat Strike, 51
Tydings, Joseph P., 62
Tydings, Millard E., 37-8

U. S. News and World Report,
    78

University of Baltimore, 14, 16, 32
Urban Renewal, 34, 45, 105

Vance, Cyrus, 87
Vice Presidential Campaign, 13, 77-100
Vice Presidents of the Past, 100-5
Vietnam Moratorium, 109, 110

Wallace, George, 100, 125
Ward, C. D., 147, 152
Ware, Gilbert, 46, 60, 86, 151
Washington Daily News, 49

Washington Post, 48, 90, 91, 97, 99, 109, 123, 128-31, 143
Washington Star, 48
Welcome, Verda, 60
White, George, 46, 96-9, 133
Wilkens, Roy, 57, 122, 149
Wilkinson, Bud, 145
Wolff, Jerome, 148
Woods, Rose Mary, 71, 140

Young, Whitney, 57

Zoning Board of Appeals, Baltimore County, 27